Cric
Inside the Game

Rob Steen

Published in 1998 by Icon Books Ltd,
Grange Road, Duxford, Cambridge CB2 4QF
e-mail: icon@mistral.co.uk

Distributed in the UK, Europe, Canada, South Africa and Asia
by the Penguin Group:
Penguin Books Ltd, 27 Wrights Lane, London W8 5TZ

Published in Australia in 1998 by Allen & Unwin Pty Ltd,
PO Box 8500, 9 Atchison Street, St Leonards, NSW 2065

Text copyright © 1998 Rob Steen

The author has asserted his moral rights

No part of this book may be reproduced in any form, or by any
means, without prior permission in writing from the publisher

ISBN 1 84046 031 8

Series edited by Sport and Leisure Books Ltd
Layout and illustrations: Zoran Jevtic, Audiografix
Cover design by Zoran Jevtic and Jeremy Cox
Photographs supplied by Colorsport

Printed and bound in Great Britain by
Biddles Ltd, Guildford and King's Lynn

CONTENTS

INTRODUCTION	4
WHAT AND WHEN	6
HOW	71
WHY	99
DREAM TEAMS	163
BE AN INSTANT BLUFFER	169
About the author	172
Index	174

INTRODUCTION

A beginner's guide to cricket. In 40,000 words. With lots of pictures. My initial response, I readily confess, was one of extreme snottiness and downright cowardice. Might just as well ask a chap to boil the Old Testament down into a comic. Then I noticed the gauntlet lying at my feet.

The aim of this book is straightforward yet far from simple. Namely, to provide as many answers as possible to anyone with a burgeoning fascination for (or even the slightest, vaguest, teensiest interest in) cricket. The trouble with cricket is that its seemingly endless complexities and apparent passion for anachronistic traditions alienate many would-be aficionados. What follows is an attempt to ease your anxiety, de-furrow those brows and keep the aspidistra flying. To explain, enlighten and, I hope, enthuse. In short, to woo.

The problem with all this is not so much where to begin as where to end. I have tried, to the best of my ability, to achieve a degree of balance between comprehensiveness and comprehension. To this end, the book is divided into various sections: WHAT AND WHEN deals with the principles and evolution of the game, the rules and the terminology; HOW with its techniques; WHY with its history. There is also a records section and an Instant Bluffer's Guide, together with a guide to the giants and a day-by-day account of one of the most memorable and heroic of all cricket matches. A contest that vividly captured the game's skills, its tactics, its emotions, its characters, and, best of all, its utterly preposterous uncertainty.

For their help, clues, tips and shoves in the general vicinity of the right direction (wittingly or otherwise), I would like to thank Everyone At Icon,

Rab MacWilliam (thanks for the gauntlet but I still can't warm to The Gooners), Gordon Vince (Number-Cruncher), Sir Derek Birley (Agent Provocateur), Peter Wynne-Thomas (Digger Supreme), Simon Wilde (Quote Master), Huw Richards (Sounding-Board and Slapper-Down of Daft/Duff/Ludicrous Concepts), Mr and Mrs Apple Mac. And, of course, my infinitely superior half Anne (who would advise you not to read any further, but then what do they know that cricket know not?).

Heartfelt thanks, above all, to Laura, Josef and Bun-in-Oven: for the incentive.

Rob Steen
Alexandra Palace
June 1998

Inside the Game   **WHAT AND WHEN**

AIMS

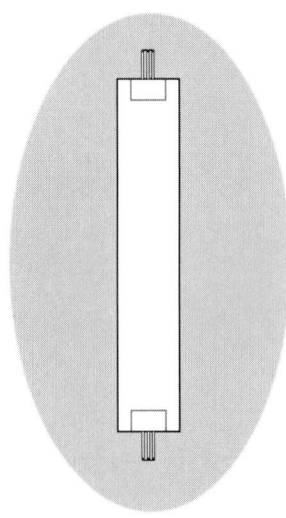

The pitch (overhead view)

Depending on your point of view, cricket is either the most fun you can have with a ball without stroking it or, as one sceptic put it many moons ago, 'organised loafing'. The world's least frantic outdoor game is also, at first glance, its most complex. How could it be otherwise when it is eminently possible for a match to consume five days and still fail to produce a conclusive result? Then again, cricket and life have a lot more in common than most sports.

In Test and first-class cricket, the senior professional codes, a match comprises two teams of eleven players *batting* and *bowling* for two *innings* apiece (if necessary), each of six hours' duration, for up to four or five days. The *bowler* bowls the ball overarm (see **Delivery**) from either end of a strip of turf (the *pitch*) measuring 22 yards long by 10 feet wide. Facing him is a *batsman* (or *striker*) armed with a wooden bat, whose objective is twofold: (a) to *defend* his *wicket* (three wooden stumps inserted into the ground at both ends of the pitch, topped with a pair of *bails* and minded by a *wicketkeeper*, whose prime function is to collect any balls missed); (b) score as many *runs* as possible (or required) before a *bowler* can get him *out* by *taking* his *wicket* (see **Dismissals**).

The bowlers (aka the *attack*) bowl alternate *overs* from different ends comprising six *balls* or *deliveries* (now standard after fluctuating between four and eight for more than two centuries). The batsman is entitled to hit the ball in front of or behind the wicket, to his right (the *off side* if right-handed) or left (the *leg side* or *on side*). Runs are added to the team total either by running between each set of stumps as often as practicable while a

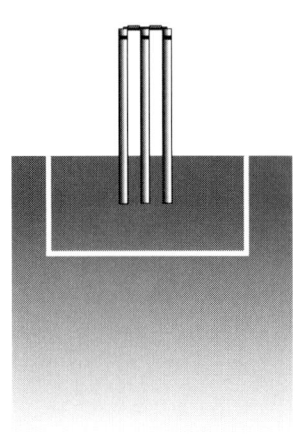

The stumps/wicket

6

fielder attempts to retrieve the ball (there are always two batsmen *in* at any juncture, so the *non-striker* must run too) or by striking the ball beyond the *boundary* (see **Boundary**). The most common currency is the *single*, i.e. one run.

Each team's innings comprises up to eleven individual innings, but since two batsmen must be batting at all times, only ten wickets need be taken by the *fielding* side. When one team is *all out*, or *declares* its innings closed (see **Declaration**), the opposition goes in, and so on. The exception is when the side batting second trails by a wide margin, in which case it may be asked to go in again (see **Follow-On**). All being well, the contest will be conducted on a neatly-mowed field devoid of hills and hollows.

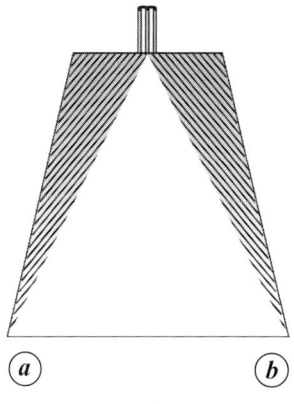

a) Off side (to right-hander)
b) Leg side (to right-hander)

Victory is achieved by bowling the opposition out twice and aggregating more runs, which may mean meeting a target of runs in the final innings. The margin may either be a number of runs or a number of wickets (the number still to *fall* at the moment the winning run is made). In nigh-on 1,400 Test matches to March 1998, only once has a team won by one run (West Indies v Australia, Adelaide 1993). If one side makes more runs in one innings than the opposition manage in two, they are said to have won by *an innings* and a certain number of runs. Failing that, the result is a *draw*, unless the scores are level and the side batting last is all out, in which case the outcome is a *tie*. In Tests to date, there have been but two ties.

Essentially the film of the book (and often a cartoon at that), *limited-overs* – or *one-day* – cricket is restricted to one innings per side, each lasting for a maximum number of overs (usually 50), with bowlers limited to a maximum number of overs (usually 10): this is also the format practised in an increasingly large percentage of games at amateur level. Since there is no need to take all 10 wickets, stalemates are rare. When teams achieve the same number of runs the issue is decided by their respective scoring rates (runs per over); if they still cannot be separated, the outcome – with scant regard for the correct terminology – is deemed to be a tie. Time-honoured roles, moreover, are reversed: bowlers defend, batsmen attack. Taking wickets is less important than restricting runs.

Given a pitch equally well-disposed to bowlers and batsmen, plus a kind hand from Pluvius, the following constitutes a rough guide to the various totals a batting side may achieve in its first innings, together with a similar barometer for individual performances.

Test/First-class
400-plus: probable victory and insurance against defeat; 300-plus: competitive; 225–75: iffy; 150–200: dodgy; 0–100: expect at least one day off

One-day (50 overs)
300-plus: virtually invincible; 250–75: solid; 200–plus: useful; 150–75: shaky; 100–49: ominous; 0–99: humiliation

Individual batting (runs in an innings)
400+ Jaw-dropping; 300+ Huge; 200+ Towering; 150+ Big; 100+ Substantial; 75+ Sizeable; 50+ Adequate; 30+ Moderate; 10+ Diminutive; 1–9 Scornful; 0 Pitiful

Individual bowling (wickets in an innings)
10: Perfect; 8+ Heroic; 6+ Superb; 5 Bloody Good; 3+ Damn Useful; 2 Um, Well; 1 Start Panicking;

0: Make Alternative Arrangements For Next Game

There is, of course, one rider to all this: context is all. The scoreboard, as Neville Cardus once observed, 'is an ass'.

ASHES, THE

Symbolic name for the prize at stake in Test matches between England and Australia since 1882. Housed in a tiny urn, the 'ashes' are purportedly those of English cricket, commemorating the national team's first defeat on home soil. *Sporting Times* published a mock obituary : 'In affectionate remembrance of English cricket which died at The Oval on 29th August, 1882. Deeply lamented by a large circle of sorrowing friends and acquaintances. RIP. NB – The body will be cremated and the ashes taken to Australia.' During England's tour of Australia that winter, the Hon. William Clarke and Lady Clarke staged a social match at their Rupertswood estate thirty miles outside Melbourne, after which the lady of the house burnt a bail and deposited the ashes in a wooden urn, which she duly presented to the tourists' captain, the Hon. Ivo Bligh, Earl of Darnley. A few weeks later, Anne Fletcher, the wife of the secretary of the Paddington Cricket Club in Sydney, made a crimson velvet bag and dispatched it to Bligh. 'Many thanks for the pretty little bag', he replied. 'The ashes shall be consigned to it forthwith and always kept there in memory of the great match.' Recently, however, it has emerged that the ashes were probably the remnants of a veil.

Ashes winner: David Gower

Bligh kept bag and urn at his Cobham Hall estate in Kent until his death in 1927, whereupon Lady Darnley sent the latter to Lord's for safekeeping:

it can now be found in the Memorial Gallery at Lord's, never to be removed; not even when Australia are the (purely theoretical) holders, as is generally the case. On average, the countries meet every two years for a *series* (or *rubber*) comprising five or six Tests, taking turns to play host; in order to regain the Ashes, the series must be won outright, whereas the 'holders' need only draw it to retain possession. It was a good thing the urn was not at stake for the one-off Centenary Test of 1980, an occasion marred by seemingly needless delays and safety-first play. 'In affectionate remembrance of English cricket which died at Lord's on September 2, 1980, aged one hundred', began a letter in *Wisden Cricket Monthly*. 'The body will be re-cremated and sent to the home of bureaucracy, officialdom, and the tactics of defensive unadventurous cricket.'

Between 1989 and 1997 Australia took five rubbers in succession, a twentieth-century record, winning seventeen Tests to England's five. Suitably emboldened, the 1997 touring party requested permission to take the urn back Down Under; Lord's, typically, was not for turning (see **MCC**).

AVERAGES

The ultimate measure of individual performance, albeit more a celebration of tradition than precision. A batting average is calculated by *dividing* the number of runs scored by the number of completed innings (i.e. those in which the batsman is out). A bowling average is calculated by dividing the number of runs conceded by the number of wickets taken. What neither take into account are the circumstances (Australia's Bill

Johnston, a cunning seamer and negligible batsman, once averaged more than 100 on a tour of England, mostly by dint of *not outs*). In a laudable attempt to produce something a little less one-dimensional, Ted Dexter, the broad-thinking former England captain, formulated the world ratings (now the Coopers & Lybrand world rankings), a highly complex system of computerised evaluation that takes into account the standard of the opposition, the state of the game and the condition of the pitch. Too subjective for most tastes, sadly.

The best-known average is 99.94 – Don Bradman's phenomenal batting average in Tests. In his final innings against England at the Oval in 1948, he needed just 4 runs to finish with a career average of 100; he was bowled second ball for 0.

BALL

Compressed-granulated cork encased by dyed red leather stitched with flax twine (the *seam*); weight 5 1/2oz (for men) or 5oz (for women). First referred to by Milton's nephew, Edward Phillips, in *The Mysteries of Love* (1658): a woman fears that her lover will one day say, 'Would my eyes had been beat out of my head with a cricket ball the day before I saw thee.' Even then it conjured images of extreme hardness. The oldest known ball, said to date from around 1780, was found in 1995, at a house in Lewes, Sussex, inside a woman's shoe. Depending on the angle required, the ball is propelled at the batsman from either *over* (with the stumps next to the bowling hand) or *round* the wicket (the opposite side). The point at which it lands on the pitch is where it *pitches*.

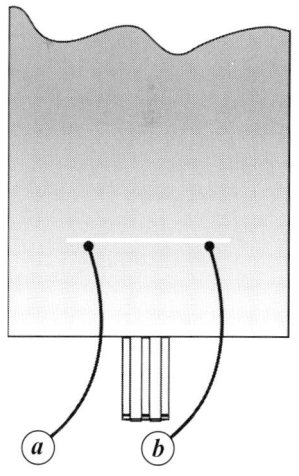

a) Over the wicket (right-handed bowler)
b) Round the wicket

BAT

Onomatopoeic. 'A club to strike the ball with, at the play called Cricket' according to N. Bailey's *An Universal Etymological Dictionary* (1721), the word's first known appearance in a reference work. Made of willow, with a smooth face and an angled back, it measures 4 1/4 inches across, tapers into a handle and was originally curved at the end. A biblical tableau in Queen Mary's Psalter, an illuminated manuscript in the British Library said to date from the early fourteenth century, depicts Cain and Abel wielding shepherd's crooks while the latter holds a ball roughly 4 inches in diameter. The inscription cites them as playing 'festes' with 'pelottes', a ball (from *pelotter*, another French word for 'frapper', to hit). Hence the conclusion drawn by John Eddowes, in *The Language of Cricket*, that this most English of games may well have been exported from across the Channel by armies defending the king's hard-won territorial possessions. Perish the thought.

One or two ragamuffins, unsurprisingly, have extracted the urine. In 1771, Thomas 'Shock' White came out to bat for Reigate, wrote John Nyren, with a bat which 'being the width of the stumps, effectively defended his wicket from the bowler'. Nyren's club, the then all-powerful Hambledon, objected to this strenuously and demanded a width restriction of 4 1/4 inches, which became law in 1774. Two centuries later, at Perth in 1979, Dennis Lillee shamelessly decided to obtain the maximum publicity for his new invention, the aluminium bat, by brandishing it as he went out to bat for Australia in front of the TV cameras. After a couple of clanging blows, Mike Brearley, the England captain, objected, citing the damage it might do the ball: Lillee, livid, flung it away, whereupon the offending item was withdrawn and banned. Until then, the *Laws* had never actually specified that the bat be made of wood.

BATTING ORDER

Most obstructive first, least resilient last. Generally speaking, after the openers come the so-called 'strokeplayers', aka the middle-order (3 to 6, including any *all-rounders*, i.e. those able to bat and bowl with equal or near-equal facility); the wicketkeeper follows and the bowlers (*tailenders* or *rabbits*) bring up the rear. That said, it is not unknown for a wicketkeeper to open an innings, India's Farokh Engineer and England's Alec Stewart being two notable examples. A captain may juggle according to the state of the game: if quick runs are needed, he may promote one of his lustier hitters, which might even mean one of the bowlers.

Conversely, he may even reverse the order (see **Declaration**). 'On several occasions I was compelled to rearrange our order as a matter of tactics because of the state of the wicket', reflected Australia's nonpareil, Don Bradman. 'It almost invariably succeeded. Some were unkind enough to suggest that my purpose was to avoid batting on a wet wicket. Of course it was; but only because such avoidance was necessary in the interests of the team.'

BOUNDARY

(a) perimeter of the playing field, denoted by rope, fence and/or advertising hoarding, anything from 70 to 100 yards from the pitch; (b) unit of scoring for shots that cross the boundary. Until 1910, the batsman gained four runs unless he succeeded in driving the ball clean out of the ground, which brought six; on the recommendation of the Advisory County Cricket Committee, any blow clearing the boundary was subsequently worth six. The most boundaries in a first-class innings is 68 (all fours), by Percy Perrin during his 343 not out for Essex v Derbyshire at Chesterfield, 1904. The highest score made without the aid of a single boundary is 103 (A. Hill, Orange Free State v Griqualand West, Bloemfontein, South Africa,1976–7).

BUMP BALL

If the batsman squeezes the ball into the ground, whereupon it loops to a fielder, a catch should not be awarded. One incident of this nature played a catalytic role in cricket history. Brisbane 1946, the first postwar Ashes Test: an ailing Bradman, on what many assumed would be his final appearance for Australia, had made his way unconvincingly to 18 when he edged Alec Bedser towards the slips; Jack Ikin claimed the catch. Much to the chagrin of the England fielders, Bradman refused to accept Ikin's word and awaited the umpire's decision. The ruling was a bump ball, Bradman went on to make 187 and duly led the all-conquering 1948 tour to the mother country, his very presence giving the game a timely and lasting boost.

CAPTAINCY

'On Friday I watched J.M. Brearley directing his fielders very carefully', a reader wrote to *Wisden Cricket Monthly* in 1981. 'He then looked up at the sun and made a gesture which suggested it should move a little squarer. Who is this man?' Few and far between as they are, captains of

Cricket

Brearley's calibre have their own unique mystique, and are duly accorded the sort of reverence normally reserved for Popes and winners of the Nobel Peace Prize. And rightly so. After all, we are talking about the second toughest job in professional sport (cleaning a mud-wrestler's kit beats it by a nose).

No other game, certainly, demands so much from one man. The captain of a cricket team, after all, is player, manager, psychologist and nurse, responsible for his own performance as well as those of his colleagues. There can be no more shining exponent of this paternalistic role than the sagacious Frank Worrell. As the West Indies' first regular black captain, he insisted on Trinidadians rooming with Jamaicans, and Barbadians with Guyanans, bringing home to his colleagues the need to bury inter-island rivalries for the good of black unity: only then did they begin to convert individual talent into collective profit.

The cap fits: Mike Brearley

Once the appropriate selection committee has chosen the team (a process in which he may take no direct part) it is the captain who makes all the major decisions: who bats when, who bowls when, who fields where; whether to bat or bowl first (see **Toss**); when to take the new ball (see **New Ball**) or close an innings (see **Declaration**); even what roller to use on the pitch (see **Pitch**). Accordingly, it is he who takes the plaudits and carries the can. 'Dear Brearley', one of his less ardent admirers wrote, 'There is an old Italian proverb: if you want to know a fish is bad look at its head.' More perceptive was the Australian Richie Benaud, one of the shrewdest of all Test captains. 'Captaincy', he reckons, 'is 90% luck and 10% skill ... but for heaven's sake, don't try it without that little 10%.'

There are two schools of thought pertaining to the selection of a captain: while the Australians are traditionally adamant he should be picked from among the best eleven players available, the English are usually quite content for him to justify his place purely on the grounds of his ability to lead. Which is why Brearley, a specialist batsman who failed to muster a single century in 66 innings for England, was able to build himself such an enduring reputation. 'It is true that captaincy at best is often a matter of intuition', he wrote in the introduction to his seminal treatise, *The Art of Captaincy*. 'The heart must be in the right place, but so must the mind and its attention to detail.' Derek Underwood, his former Test teammate, summed up the bafflement of lesser mortals with admirable succinctness: 'Why do so many players *want* to be captain?'

CENTURY

Aka a *hundred*, an individual, partnership or team score of 100 or more; if you're Brian Lara, you can even score a quintuple century. A century is the batsman's main objective, the average ETA three to four hours. The gathering of the 100th/200th/300th run is a traditional cue for applause; spectators are even polite enough to clap half-centuries, 150s etc. It is even *de rigeur* for fielders to join the acclaim.

CLOTHING (see also EQUIPMENT)

Eighteenth Century:
Three-cornered (or jockey) hats, often embroidered with silver/gold lace; frilled shirts; silk stockings; buckled shoes; breeches. Hambledon players wore sky-blue coats with buttons.

Cricket

1800–50:
Trousers replace breeches; tall beaver hats in black or white (soon replaced by flannel caps and straw hats); shirts lose frills but gain high collars; bow ties; belts; black Oxford shoes; short white jackets.

1850–80:
Influenced by I Zingari CC, club colours emerge, often as ribbons draped around white bowler hats or club caps; coloured shirts also worn to denote club, with either spots, stripes or checks (All England XI wear white shirts with pink spots).

1880–95:
White shirts with starched fronts; bow ties with turned down collars; white buckskin boots; white flannel trousers; caps ease out bowler hats.

1895–1977:
Bow ties, turned-down collars out.

1977 to date:
Coloured shirts, flannels and V-necked sweaters re-introduced for limited-overs matches only, replete with matching pads; training shoes replace boots; baseball caps in vogue; sunglasses for fielders; zinc cream daubed on face as further protection from sun (and holes in ozone layer). Players identified by numbers and names on shirts in one-day games only.

CRIMES and MISDEMEANOURS

Bribery
For all those umbilical associations with gambling, it took more than a century for cricket to confront its first major bribes scandal. The charges surfaced early in 1995, four months after Pakistan had

beaten Australia in Karachi, a match decided in highly improbable fashion when the hosts' final pair added 57, the highest last-wicket stand to win a Test. The decisive runs, moreover, were byes, emanating from a missed stumping by the most reliable wicketkeeper in the business.

The match was played on a ground where the hosts had never lost, in a city where illegal bookies are said to exert more than a modicum of power. On the fourth evening, or so claimed the Australian batsman, Mark Waugh, he received a phone call from the Pakistan captain, Salim Malik, offering him money. The conversation was overheard by Waugh's hotel roommate, Tim May. Shane Warne further claimed that he had visited Malik's room and been offered US$200,000 to bowl badly on the final day. Fearing, they said, for their safety, May, Warne and Waugh declined an invitation to return to the scene of the crime and reiterate their testimony. Since then, a leading Australian player is said to have been fined for providing bookmakers with sensitive information (i.e. the physical and mental well-being of his colleagues). In the meantime, Rashid Latif and Aamir Sohail both accused their compatriots of bribery: the former promptly announced his retirement, while the latter was suspended; both, curiously, have captained Pakistan since recanting. A number of one-day matches have also come under scrutiny, but the Karachi crisis rumbles on. In 1998, the Pakistani government ordered an independent investigation; whether anything concrete ever emerges is open to considerable doubt.

Throwing

Aka chucking. Unusual now, an epidemic in the 1950s almost brought the game to a standstill. Granted, it doesn't sound that awful. Guilt, after

Cricket

all, is nothing more than a bent arm (at the point a bowler delivers). Indeed, many of the 100-odd cases in first-class history have been intentional jokes, such as when England's David Gower threw the last ball of the 1986 Test at Trent Bridge with New Zealand requiring one to win. What offends is not so much the potential for enhanced accuracy as for extra speed and bounce. The possibility, in other words, of grievous bodily harm.

Not that fast bowlers are the only offenders. A tricky, highly subjective decision customarily left to the judgement of the square-leg umpire – who has more time to scrutinise and much the better vantage point – it was hard to blame the Sri Lankans for almost creating an international incident in 1996 when Darrell Hair no-balled their off-spinner, Muttiah Muralitharan, from the bowler's end.

The inherent difficulties are amply illustrated by the case of Charles Christopher Griffith. In 1962, Nari Contractor, the captain of India, sustained a fractured skull and lay close to death after ducking into a ball from Griffith, the fiery Barbadian speedster; in the second innings, Griffith, who was so distraught he had begged not to bowl, returned reluctantly to the attack only to be *called* for throwing. An understandable – if erroneous – connection was made. For the remainder of his career, 'although Contractor knew I was guiltless', Griffith was persecuted, his action endlessly monitored and questioned. He was called again, once in a Test against England; so blatant could his transgressions appear, one photograph made him look as if he was lining up a treble 20. To the end, he insisted he was unaware of any kink, nor guilty of intent. As long ago as 1900, the county captains saw it as a vexing matter. Amid what was

Chucked around: Charlie Griffith

perceived as the first throwing crisis, they joined forces in the wake of a match in which James Phillips, the Australian umpire, had repeatedly no-balled Arthur Mold of Lancashire; Mold retired the following season after his next encounter with Phillips, who pulled him up 10 times in 16 overs. 'Personally', averred Pelham Warner, the Middlesex and England captain, 'Mold was the nicest of men, and I am certain he never intentionally threw.' From 1908 to 1952, claimed the historian Gerald Brodribb, not one bowler was called in English first-class cricket, but that didn't mean, of course, that everyone was squeaky clean. Wary of the consequences such an action might have on the offender's livelihood, some umpires turned a blind eye; others looked away for political reasons.

In 1951, when Frank Chester, then the game's best-known umpire, wanted to call Cuan McCarthy, the South African fast bowler, Pelham Warner (by now Sir Pelham as well as MCC president, and a man distinctly unused to getting no for an answer) said he would rather he desisted. 'These people', reasoned Sir Pelham, 'are our guests.' At Lord's in 1960, Syd Buller, the most esteemed umpire of his generation, was not quite so hospitable. Having seen his colleague, Frank Lee, call another South African quick bowler, Geoff Griffin (who was called by no fewer than ten different umpires during his ill-starred career), Buller heaped insult upon injury in the exhibition match that followed, calling the hapless Griffin for failing to inform the batsman that he would be bowling underarm.

Coincidentally or not, the most almighty furore exploded in the winter of 1958–9, while England were getting a thorough going-over from an Australian side liberally sprinkled with bowlers of

Cricket

dubious persuasion. 'The winning or losing of the Ashes is a small matter compared with "the greatest catastrophe in cricket"', wrote E. W. Swanton in the *Daily Telegraph*, quoting Sir Donald Bradman. Nor did the Don stop there: it was he who led the clean-up campaign. 'If they stop throwing', asserted Tommy Andrews, the erstwhile Australian Test player, 'cricket in Australia will die.' Happily, he was wide of the mark.

Not that the English could afford to throw too many stones. Peter Loader and Tony Lock, mainsprings of the Surrey team that won seven consecutive county championships between 1952 and 1958, were both pursued by persistent allegations; indeed, Lock, a left-arm spinner whose faster ball once prompted a victim to wonder 'was I bowled or run out?', was 'called' in the Caribbean. Only when he saw film of himself did he acknowledge that his accusers may have had a point.

Sometimes, though, it is possible to have sympathy. Take Jeff Jones, Glamorgan's pacy left-armer, a valuable member of the England attack in 1968 but finished with the game within twelve months: Tony Lewis, his county skipper, advised him that his action made it impossible for him to be selected with a clear conscience. Then there was Harold Rhodes, the former Derbyshire (and briefly England) opening bowler who claimed an accident of birth made it merely appear as if he was throwing (much like Muralitharan). 'If they re-write the Laws and say that double-jointed people must not be allowed to play the first-class game', he mused bitterly, 'well, fair enough.'

Beamer
Aka high full-toss. Fast delivery that flies straight

WELL I NEVER !

The Kennington Oval in South London, venue of England's highest-ever Test score (903 for 7 declared v Australia, 1938), was used as a prisoner-of-war camp during the Second World War.

Two players were sent off for fighting during a 1996 club match between Buckley and Shotton in north Wales. When wicketkeeper Marcel Carrino floored a simple catch, the reprieved batsman, Andy Cummings, began to taunt him and a brawl ensued. The umpires pondered abandoning the game but continued after dismissing the pair for 'ungentlemanly conduct'.

Zimbabwean wicketkeeper Wayne James will doubtless look back on Matabeleland's 1996 match against Mashonaland Central Districts in Bulawayo with a mixture of passion and scorn for statistics. Having equalled the world record for victims in an innings, he was dismissed for 99, whereupon he broke the world mark for victims in a match and proceeded to win the contest with 99 not out. Only one player in first-class history had previously made two 99s in the same game.

Four races on the card at Warwick in July 1996 were named after members of the Indian touring team: the Anil Kumble Maiden Handicap, the Sanjay Manjrekar Selling Handicap, the Sachin Tendulkar Maiden Stakes and the Mohammad Azharuddin Handicap. Pity the tourists were prohibited from betting.

Like great-grandfather like great-grandson: In 1996, playing for Brooke Under-18s against Norfolk foes Loddon, Nick Causton, 14, took six wickets with successive balls, albeit not in the same over (two came from the last two balls from one over, the other four at the start of the next). Seventy-four years earlier, Sidney Causton achieved a similar feat. The commemorative ball now resides with Nick.

Cuba's first official cricket match, between Havana CC and the Cayman Islands in January 1997, was a triumph for adaptability. Played at the Eduardo Saborit Stadium, a disused greyhound track outside the capital, a matting pitch had conveniently been found there, rolled up in the corner of an office: it was snapped up for $30, a mop, two bottles of detergent and a crate of beer.

Thirty inhabitants of Aurangabad were estimated to have gone on hunger strike in 1997 after the Indian selectors dropped former captain and star batsman Mohammad Azharuddin.

B.B. Nimbalkar must have fancied his chances of breaking Don Bradman's (then) world-record score of 452 when he went to lunch at Poona, India in 1948 with 443 not out against his name. Unfortunately, Kathiawar, the opposing team, decided that Maharashtra's total of 826 for 4 was already too daunting and abruptly conceded the match.

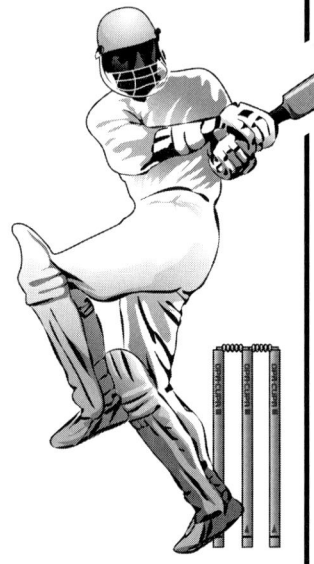

John Hague was doing his level best to prevent a boundary while playing for Horncastle in Bardney, Lincolnshire, when he was knocked unconscious by an out-of-control hang glider. The headline? 'Bad Flight Stops Play'.

at the batsman's chest or head without bouncing. Habitually followed by a 'whoops, she slipped' from the sheepish bowler, even if that was precisely his intention. Accidental or not, the penalty is a no-ball.

Ball-tampering
Controversial and firmly traditional gambit, against the rules but largely tolerated, until recently. A bowler may be perfectly at liberty to shine the ball on his crotch (in an effort to obtain swing), but tampering with it is another matter entirely. In order to persuade an old ball to deviate through the air or off the pitch, a bowler may seek to damage or unpick the seam, with or without a little bit of help from colleagues, bottle-tops or sturdy fingernails. Or, for that matter, a pocketful of dirt, as the England captain, Mike Atherton, was infamously accused of doing during a Test against South Africa at Lord's in 1994. The upshot – of what came to be known as 'Pocketgate' – was a fine for the miscreant, not for using the dirt to keep the ball dry (or so he claimed) but for fibbing: he initially denied all knowledge of the 'alien' substance.

In 1921, Johnny Douglas, the England captain, threatened to report Arthur Mailey, Australia's wily leg-spinner, for illegally employing resin to help him grip the ball, only to change his tune rather abruptly when Mailey pointed out that Douglas's thumbnail was worn to the quick from illegally lifting the seam. There are those, furthermore, such as England's Angus Fraser, who advocate picking the seam: in a game in which most of the rules conspire against the bowlers, he regards it as a means of at least partially balancing the books.

Double standards, as ever, are omnipresent. In 1992, Waqar Younis, Pakistan's prodigious pace spearhead, was hounded mercilessly by the English media for alleged tampering, even though the evidence (i.e. the ball itself), intriguingly enough, was safely locked away in a Lord's safe and never exhibited publicly. Two years earlier, when the umpire, John Holder, reprimanded the England captain, Graham Gooch, for a similar misdeed, the matter caused scarcely a ripple; at the time of writing, other than as a *third umpire*, Holder had yet to stand in another Test.

Sledging

Verbal harassment designed to disrupt the batsman's concentration, freely indulged in by bowler, fielders and wicketkeeper alike. The scope of the term has widened appreciably: originally, a sledger was anyone with the poor form to be indiscreet in the presence of a woman. According to Ian Chappell, the former captain of Australia, the term was coined in the 1960s, from a salty description of a party's failure by his one-time international teammate, Grahame Corling, in front of a waitress. 'It's all fucked up', exclaimed Corling, who was duly informed he possessed the subtlety of a sledgehammer. Percy Sledge's 'When A Man Loves A Woman' was riding high in the pop charts at the time, hence Corling's instant nickname of 'Sledge'. That said, the tactic is timeless.

Ace sledger: Merv Hughes

Bouncer

A legitimate, occasionally exhilarating form of attack, questionable when deployed solely for

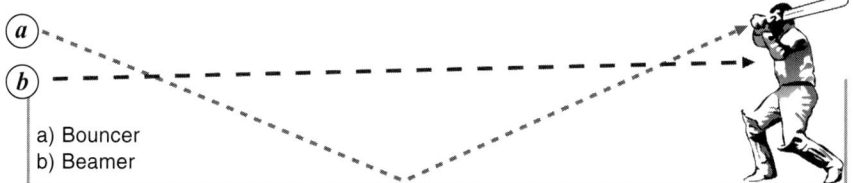

a) Bouncer
b) Beamer

purposes of intimidation, reprehensible when employed to remove stubborn tailenders. Can be dangerous even when not done to excess. Playing for Broxtowe against Nottinghamshire rivals Gladstone in 1996, opener John Shaw, 47, suffered a fatal brain haemorrhage after being struck on the head. In order to encourage moderation and reduce injuries, the International Cricket Council decreed in the early 1990s that bowlers be limited to one bouncer per batsman per over. The West Indian fast bowlers, comfortably the most dangerous exponents, were convinced they were being victimised by a hierarchy eager to revive the Anglo-Australian duopoly, and not entirely without justification.

Appealing
Legal and often just. If there is no appeal and the batsman declines to take the law into his own hands (see **Walking**) it is the only means by which the umpire can be obliged to make a ruling on a dismissal. At the same time, however, appeals are frequently made solely to unsettle the batsman, regardless of their legitimacy. The modern practice of appealing for everything is widely frowned on – especially when the howzats emanate from fielders in no position to judge – yet often reaps results. It is not unknown for susceptible umpires to be swayed into error by the sheer orchestrated vociferousness of the appellants. Equally, this may harden his resolve not to 'give' anything. The proposal that frequent offenders be disciplined with yellow and red cards *à la* football has much to commend it.

Running on the pitch
After delivery, a fast bowler may follow through on the line of the stumps, or close to them, scuffing up the pitch and hence (potentially) helping the spinners extract more turn. Regardless of intent,

the misdemeanour becomes a crime after two warnings from the umpire; one more transgression and the guilty party is banned from bowling for the rest of the innings.

Slow over rates
Overrated. In the 1880 Test between England and Australia, nearly 500 overs were bowled in less than 3 days; at Delhi in 1981, India and England delivered 343 in 5. That said, Parkinson's Law was not the only reason why the rate declined so markedly. Nor, for that matter, was the preponderance of fast bowlers with seemingly endless run-ups (India and England boasted four spinners between them). Given the huge surge in the frequency of international fixtures over the past quarter of a century, captains have more reason than ever to defend a leisurely tempo as a sensible means of conserving energy, not least under an enervating sun. Fewer overs, counter the critics, mean the public are short-changed, a somewhat contentious theory: in tense situations, the passages between deliveries (field-changes, pep talks, consultations, the by-play between batsman and fielders) can be the most fascinating. The other main objection brooks fewer arguments: why should the fielding side be permitted to arrest the batsmen's momentum and/or prey on their concentration by effectively stopping the game? Brian Close, statistically-speaking England's most successful captain (played seven, won six, drew one), was stripped of the job in 1967 at least partly because he took delaying tactics to extremes.

Sensibly, if belatedly, a minimum daily rate was recently imposed to discourage time-wasters, along with a sliding scale of fines for non-compliance. On balance, the present requirement of 90 overs (15 per hour) seems quite adequate, although since it is unusual for the fielding side to fulfil their quota within the official playing hours, spectators can usually bank on an extra half-hour or so's free entertainment.

When India were fined 190 per cent of the individual match fee (around £475) after a Test against Sri Lanka, referee John Reid expressed his disappointment that the offenders had made little effort to hurry along. One day they took six hours to bowl 68 overs. Mind you, it was all in a worthy cause: such fines are (purportedly) earmarked for the game's developing countries.

DEAD BALL

Call made by umpire stopping play; e.g. when ball lodges in batsman's clothing or bowler inadvertently bowls ball backwards instead of forwards.

DECLARATION

If a captain feels his side has sufficient runs and would be better served devoting more time to dismissing the opposition – particularly if proceedings have been abbreviated by adverse weather – he may 'declare' an innings closed. Walter Hammond certainly evinced good grace in terminating England's first innings at the Oval in 1938: the scorebook entry, after all, read 903 for 7 declared. First authorised in 1889, albeit only on the final day of the game and in one-day matches. Progress thereafter was slow: in 1900, an innings could be declared at any stage after lunch on the second day; in 1906 it was permitted on the first day of a two-day game; in 1910 captains were empowered to declare at any juncture on the second day. Not until 1957 were they allowed to do so at any time. The timing of a declaration in the second innings of a match is critical, the tendency to err on the side of caution, especially in Tests. At Lord's in 1984, David Gower declared England's second innings at 300 for 9, leaving the West Indies a target of 342 in a minimum of 78 overs, an unheard-of rate for the last day of a Test. Not since 1948, moreover, had England lost a match after voluntarily closing their second innings. The visitors swanned home with 9 wickets and nearly 12 overs in hand.

DELIVERY

Various fiendish means by which a bowler attempts to outfox a batsman. First things first: (1) the ball must be released from within the bowling crease, a rectangular box measuring eight feet eight inches across with the stumps in the centre, taking due care not to stray from between the stumps and the return crease, the line at right-angles to the bowling crease; (2) the bowling arm must be straight at the point of release (see **Throwing** in **Crimes and Misdemeanours** section).

The target is the wicket, which comprises the *off* (to the right-handed batsman's right), *middle* and *leg* (nearest to his legs) stumps. The *line* (or direction) is critical: almost without exception, a bowler will aim between middle stump and just outside off, the reasoning being that balls on or outside the legs are easier to hit whereas those on or outside off may coax an edged shot (see **Fielders**). So, too, is the *length*: if the batsman receives a delivery that pitches too *short* he can simply step back and *pull* it away (see **Strokes**) or, if it bounces too high, let it pass; too *full* (i.e.

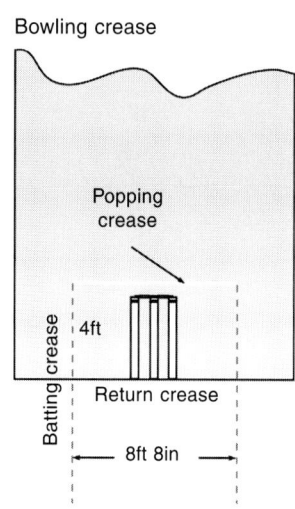

Inside the Game

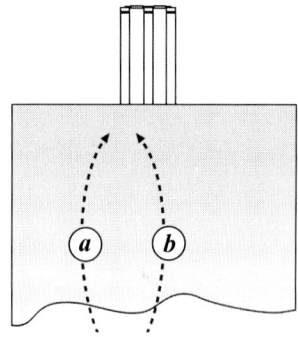

a) inswinger
b) outswinger

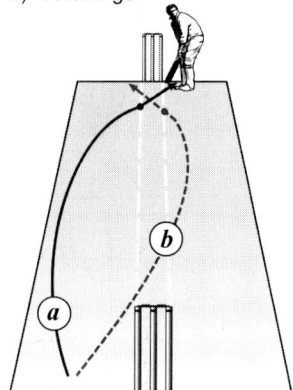

a) off-cutter
b) leg-cutter

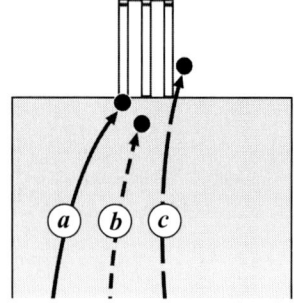

a) Yorker
b) half-volley
c) full-toss

pitches on batsman's crease), he can drive it. Between those extremes lies the *good* length, which normally obliges a defensive shot. The difference between these may be no more than an inch.

Disguising changes in *pace* and *trajectory* can be useful (spinners toss the ball in the air slowly, aiming to deceive through *flight* and *loop* as much as *turn*). The bowler's principal asset, though, is the seam, hence the expression *seamer*, used to describe someone who relies more on the interaction between pitch and stitching than speed or spin (i.e. most fast or *medium-pace* bowlers). By placing their fingers in various positions and angles alongside or across the seam, seamers and spinners alike can alter the direction the ball takes upon pitching. The following are among the most popular variations:

Fast/Medium-pace

Inswinger/outswinger – moves into or away from the batsman through the air;
Off-cutter/leg-cutter – moves in or away off the pitch;
Half-volley – pitches fractionally in front of the batsman (seldom productive);
Yorker – aimed at the base of the stumps (in 1888, A.G. Steel said he could 'find no derivation ... but we are told it came from Yorkshiremen, who were fonder of bowling this ball than any other');
Full-toss – non-bouncing (ill-advised);
Bouncer – pitched halfway down the wicket and rising towards batsman's head;
Long-hop – pitched halfway down wicket and rising towards middle of batsman's bat (not recommended).

NB: The batsman's position can determine the length. If he takes a stride forward, for instance, he can reach the ball earlier and hence turn a good-length ball into a half volley or full-toss.

Cricket

Spinners

Off-break – turns into the right-handed batsman off the pitch, away from the left-hander; spin imparted by fingers;

Leg-break – turns away from the right-hander off the pitch, into the left-hander; spin imparted by fingers and revolution of the wrist, with the ball coming out of the back of the hand;

Slow left-arm – left-armer's leg-break, spin imparted by fingers;

Arm ball – non-turning spinner (intentional);

Top-spinner – hurries straight on and bounces;

Flipper – hurries straight on and squats;

Googly – off-break masquerading as a leg-break: originally known as a 'bosie', after 'Bertie' Bosanquet, the Middlesex and England spinner who developed it in the last decade of the nineteenth century; aka a 'wrong-'un';

Chinaman – left-armer's googly (Australia); left-armer's off-break (England).

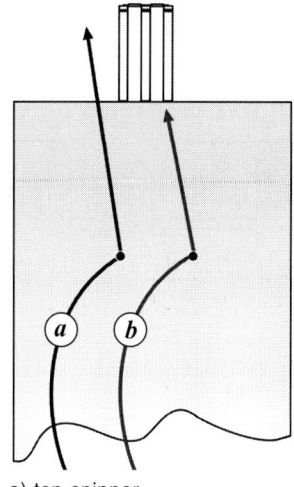

a) top-spinner
b) flipper

DISMISSAL

Various means by which the fielding side can legitimately get a batsman out, i.e. *take/grab/remove a wicket* (or, better still, *claim* a *victim*). In order of frequency, these are:

Caught: Ball goes directly from bat (or glove) to fielder without bouncing or touching the ground. If the wicketkeeper makes the catch, the batsman is said to be *caught behind*; if the bowler himself takes a *return catch*, the scorebook entry is *caught and bowled*; if the ball touches the batsman's legs en route he is said to be out to a *bat-pad* catch. Catches are either *nicked/snicked/edged/top-edged/bottom-edged/inside-edged/gloved/lobbed/ballooned/skied*. Openings of this nature are

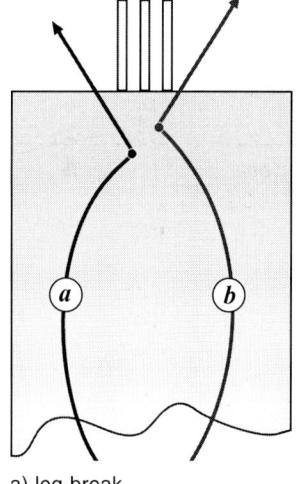

a) leg-break
b) off-break

(all diagrams relate to right-handed batsmen)

Inside the Game

known as *chances*, of which the easiest is a *dolly*. As a rule of thumb, for every catch safely held (aka *pouched/snaffled/swallowed/pocketed*), one is dropped (aka *downed/spilled/floored/squandered/fluffed/muffed*).

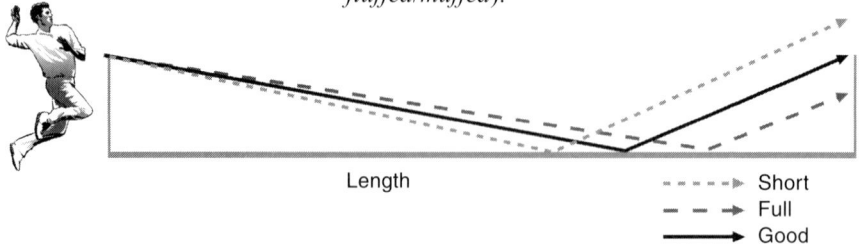

Length
- - - -▶ Short
- - -▶ Full
──▶ Good

LBW APPEAL

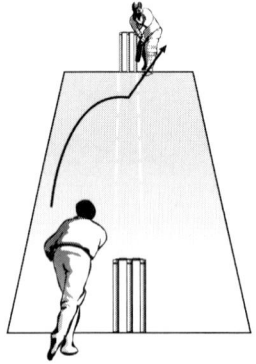

- not out (going wide)

- out

Bowled: Potentially the most thrilling sight cricket affords: ball hits one or all three stumps (it may do so via any part of the batsman's body or equipment), removing at least one bail. In the eighteenth century, this was the only way a bowler could be credited for a wicket. Batsmen so dismissed can be *yorked*, *castled*, have their stumps *plucked out* or *uprooted*, or have their *timbers shivered*.

Lbw: Aka *leg-before wicket*. Probably the most perplexing rule in sport. The ball must strike 'person, dress or equipment' in such a position that it would otherwise have hit the stumps: invariably a tricky decision for the umpire at the bowler's end, not least because it may be impossible to detect whether the ball has touched the bat first (in which case the batsman is not out). Hence the endless mutterings (and occasionally outright dissent) from aggrieved victims.

The need for such a rule was identified in the eighteenth century by 'Silver Billy' Beldham, who castigated one of the game's 'best hitters' for 'being so shabby as to put his leg in the way and take advantage of the bowlers'. At the start of the 1930s, the 'snick rule' enabled players to be adjudged lbw (or *leg-before*) even if they had touched the ball, but this was soon discarded owing to the extreme element of doubt. While spinners held sway either side of the Second World War, 'pad play' became a popular if much despised tactic, with batsmen kicking away any deliveries not pitched in line with the stumps safe in the knowledge that they could not be given out. Happily, Law 36 was eventually revamped, allowing a guilty verdict if the striker 'has made no genuine attempt to play the ball with his bat'. In 1950–1, in one of the game's most gallant moments, Walter Hadlee, the New Zealand captain, recalled England's Cyril Washbrook to the crease after disagreeing with a favourable ruling.

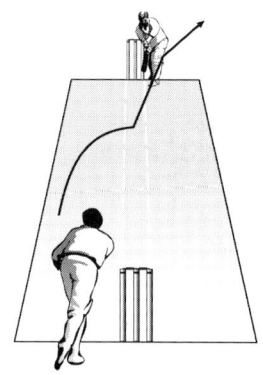
- not out (too high)

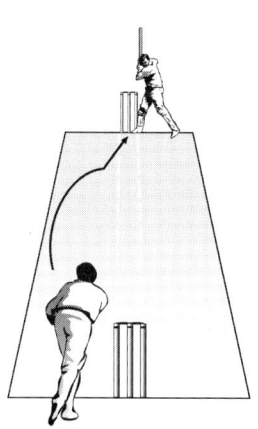
- out (no shot played)

Run out: The most spectacular of dismissals, or else the most comical. If, in attempting a run, the batsman fails to ground his bat behind the front line of the *crease* (see **popping crease**) before the bails are removed – either by a direct hit or by a colleague gathering the throw and breaking the stumps – he is run out. This may come about either through miscommunication (it is not unheard-of for both batsmen to finish up at the same end), misfortune (if the batsman's drive hits the stumps at the other end via the bowler's hand, a straying non-striker can be adjudged run out) or extraterrestrial fielding. Even so, only recently have scorecards credited the fielder, and rarely at that.

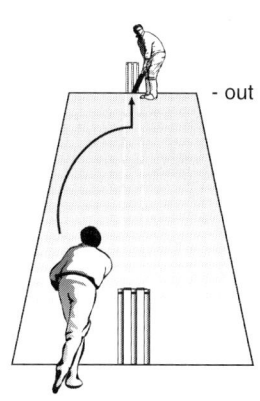
- out

It is also possible to be run out for *backing up* too far. In other words, if the non-striker fails to keep his bat grounded inside the bowler's crease until the ball is delivered – he may be attempting to steal a march with a view to attempting a quick single – the bowler is within his rights to stop and whip off

Inside the Game

RUN OUT APPEAL

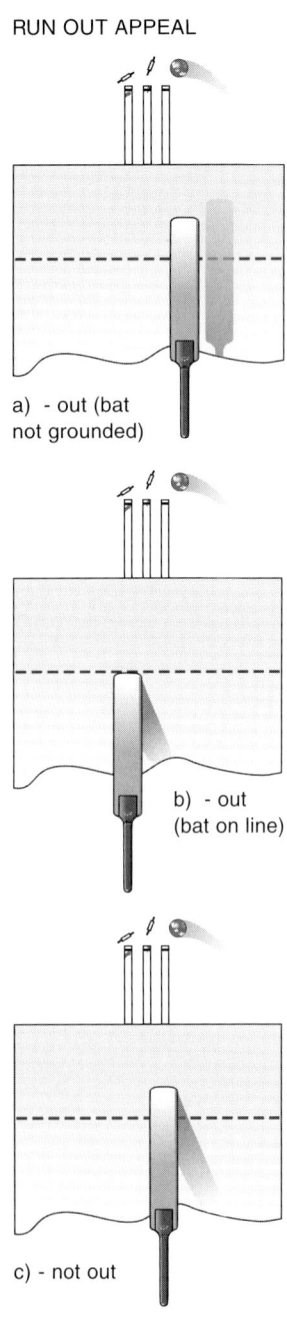

a) - out (bat not grounded)

b) - out (bat on line)

c) - not out

the bails. Custom and protocol (but not the Laws) require him first to give the offender a warning, and dismissals of this sort, thankfully, are as scarce as they are unedifying. When the West Indies' fast bowler Charlie Griffith did the dirty on Australia's Ian Redpath in 1969 – and without a warning – *Wisden Cricketers' Almanack*, the game's annual bible, drew a discreet veil over the incident.

Throwing accurately on the move is one of the game's most edifying if elusive arts, yet there were two priceless examples in as many balls as the first Test between Australia and the West Indies at Brisbane in 1960 reached its unforgettable crescendo. Australia required three to win with two wickets intact and three balls remaining when Ian Meckiff sliced Wes Hall towards the midwicket boundary. The ball pulled up a foot short, Conrad Hunte picking it up as Meckiff and Wally Grout turned for the winning runs. 'Of all the minor miracles that took place on this day I give pride of place to this one', recalled the home captain, Richie Benaud. 'Hunte was about eighty yards from the stumps when he picked up, turned and threw in one action. For Grout to be run out the ball had to go directly to [wicketkeeper] Alexander ... not to the right or left but directly to him ... thrown on the turn from eighty yards. It was a magnificent throw and as Alexander swept the bails from the stumps Grout was hurling himself towards the crease ... but still a foot out.'

Breaths had barely been caught when Lindsay Kline, the last man, played Hall's next delivery to square leg and set off for what would surely now be the conclusive run. Not until Meckiff was six yards from safety did the diminutive Joe Solomon gather the ball. Yet despite being side-on to the stumps, and therefore only having one to aim at, he hit the target. Thus was Test cricket enriched by its first tie.

Stumped: The most artistic of dismissals, albeit a comparative rarity. If a batsman is drawn forward from his crease (almost invariably by a spinner) and misses contact, the wicketkeeper can catch the ball and attempt to sweep off the bails before the batsman regains his ground. The decline of spin bowling since the Second World War is amply illustrated by the following statistic. Of Bert Oldfield's 130 victims for Australia between 1920 and 1937, 52 were stumpings, i.e. 40 per cent; of the 355 scalps snared by his successor, Rodney Marsh (1970–83), 343, i.e. 97 per cent, were catches.

Hit wicket: Exactly as it sounds. In the act of playing a shot, a batsman hits his own wicket. In the 1975 World Cup final, Roy Fredericks, the West Indies opener, hooked a six only for his back foot to slide in the morning dew, dislodging a bail. Even less fortunate was Michael Hussey, the Western Australia opener, who, during a day/night game against Queensland in 1997, launched into an off-drive and lost his grip: the bat cartwheeled over his head before landing and bouncing on to his stumps. In 1998, however, Australia's Mark Waugh inadvertently flicked the bails off with his bat after completing a stroke and was reprieved, a decision that in all probability cost South Africa victory. So enraged was Hansie Cronje, their normally placid captain, that he later admitted full responsibility for ramming a stump into the umpires' dressing-room door.

Obstructing the field: Wilful obstruction 'by word or action', e.g. preventing a catch from reaching a fielder. One of the greyer areas: can a reflex action be wilful? The most notorious example occurred in 1951 and involved Len Hutton, the heartbeat of the England order: batting against South Africa, upon seeing the ball leap shoulder-high after he had edged it into his pads, he brushed it aside as it was falling, seemingly, towards the stumps. Expecting a catch, Russell Endean, the wicketkeeper, appealed, successfully. Between 1868 and 1997, there were seventeen other recorded instances, of which two concerned one batsman, Worcestershire's T. Straw, in 1899 and 1901; conspiracy theorists might like to know that the opposition in each case were arch-enemies Warwickshire.

Dermot Reeve's antics in a county championship match for Warwickshire in 1996 provoked confusion and controversy in equal measure. To avoid being caught, he threw away his bat and used only his pad. Although the fielders were too stupified to appeal, the MCC, which declared that any repetition would be 'unacceptable', subsequently pointed out that he could have been given out for handling the ball or obstructing the field.

Handled the ball: 'It bounces up ... looks as if it's going to hit the top of the stumps ... he gives it a rather cheeky little punch.' Thus did Tony Lewis inform BBC TV viewers of Graham Gooch's indiscreet and fatal reaction to the ball from Australia's Merv Hughes that effectively sentenced England to defeat in the Lord's Test of 1993. Adhering to the letter of Law 33, umpire Dickie Bird decreed that he had 'wilfully' touched 'the ball in play with the hand not holding the bat', and that he had done so without first obtaining the 'consent of the opposite side'.

The first Englishman to be so dismissed in a Test, Gooch was less fortunate than Andrew Hilditch. In 1978–9, the Australian opener picked up the ball and handed it back to the Pakistani, Sarfraz Nawaz, a man not unduly bothered by scruples, whereupon the fast bowler's appeal was upheld. One respected BBC commentator cited such graceless behaviour as symptomatic of the modern professional. What he omitted to say was that W.G. Grace, the game's celebrated 'Champion', had achieved a similarly underhand dismissal in 1893. Between 1857 and 1996, there were forty-three infringements.

Hit the ball twice: Another vexed one. To be enforced against the batsman, according to Law 34, 'if, after the ball is struck or is stopped by any part of his person, he wilfully strikes it again with his bat or person except for the whole purpose of guarding his wicket'. Not dissimilar to obstructing the field, and even rarer. Showing a refreshing disrespect for a largely pointless regulation, not to mention an estimable command of graciousness, Anil Kumble, captaining the Rest of India against Bombay in early 1998, let Jatin Paranjpe bat on after the umpire had upheld an appeal (Paranjpe showed his gratitude by making a century). Between 1864 and 1997 there were only sixteen such offences. Test cricket still awaits its first.

Timed out: Rarer than a certifiable sighting of the Loch Ness monster. If a new batsman 'wilfully' takes more than two minutes to arrive at the wicket (the clock purportedly runs from the moment his predecessor is given out), an appeal can earn a wicket. As it is, for all that transgressions proliferate, no such appeal had ever been heard on a first-class ground until 1997, when Tripura's Hemulal Yadav, was given out during a match in India after sitting on a boundary but showing little inclination to cross it.

DOT BALL

Delivery where nothing much happens, i.e. neither a run nor a wicket. Symbolised in the scorebook by a dot. On an average day's play, a scorer can expect to record around 300 of these.

DUCK

Dismissal of a batsman without scoring. One early reference dates back to 1856, when a reporter noted that 'Wright gave another duck, making a pair': the shape of the digit zero was likened to a duck's egg. A first-ball dismissal is a golden duck (or first-baller). Aka blob, or 'failing to trouble the scorers'.

ECB

Aka the England and Wales Cricket Board, ruling body of the professional game in Britain (so why not EWCB, pray?). The most powerful voice is that of the First-Class Forum, comprising the eighteen first-class counties (one vote each), the twenty minor counties (half a vote in toto) and the MCC (half a vote). Chaired by Lord MacLaurin and based at Lord's (see **MCC**), the ECB succeeded the TCCB (Test and County Cricket Board) in 1997, the TCCB having superseded the MCC. In a salute to the counties' limitless talent for ostrich impressions, muddle-headedness and procrastination, one wit offered a fresh slant on the meaning of the acronym TCCB: Talks Complete Cock and Balderdash. The ECB's defeat in a sex discrimination case suggested traditions will be proudly maintained (see **MCC**).

EQUIPMENT

Batsmen: padded gloves, pads (to protect legs), thigh pad, forearm guard, chest guard, box (guard for genitals, worn inside a jockstrap), helmet. **Wicketkeeper:** large padded gloves, pads, box. **Fielders** (only those close to the batsman)**:** shin pads, helmet. **Spectators:** scorecard, newspaper, book, radio (with earplugs), crossword, lunch box, beverage(s).

In modern times, the most important and controversial piece of equipment has unquestionably been the helmet. Although Elias 'Patsy' Hendren pioneered a primitive model in the 1930s, it took the proliferation of bouncers in the 1970s to prompt a fully-fledged means of protecting the batsman's head. As Jeff Thomson, the Australian fast bowler, noted after the often brutal Ashes series of 1974–5, 'we were lucky nobody was killed'. In 1977, Mike Brearley took a leaf out of Hendren's book, wearing a reinforced cap and attached ear flaps; the following winter, Dennis Amiss, who had suffered at Thomson's hands himself, donned a motorcycle crash helmet, paving the way for the widespread adoption of a lighter model, complete with visor.

The tragic death of Raman Lamba in 1998 emphasised why the helmet has even become *de rigeur* for close fielders: during a club game in Bangladesh, the 38-year-old former Indian Test batsman suffered a brain haemorrhage after being struck in the head while stationed at short leg, having disdained protection. And to think that there are still those who dismiss such items as needless accoutrements.

ETON v HARROW

Anachronistic public school fixture played annually at Lord's (see **MCC**). Waning appeal saw it truncated from a two-day, two-innings-per-side match to a one-day, single-innings affair in 1982. The last player from either school to win a Test cap was Tony Pigott, the Old Harrovian who made his only appearance for England in 1984, almost forty years after the most recent Old Etonian. For the first time in 192 years, rain forced the 1997 game to be abandoned without a ball being bowled. Perhaps somebody was trying to send them a message?

EXTRAS

Runs not credited to batsmen but often debited from bowler; umpires the arbiters:

No ball: eleven different types in all, much the most common being if bowler's front heel strays over the front crease (see **Throwing** in **Crimes and Misdemeanours** section). In each case, an extra ball is added to the over and one run added or two to both the total score and the runs conceded by the bowler, in addition to any runs scored off the bat. The only way a batsman can be out off a no ball is via a run out;

Wide: delivery adjudged to be out of the batsman's reach. In first-class games this usually means beyond the width of the batting crease; in limited-overs matches the margin of error is far smaller, the aim being to prevent negative bowling. Extra ball added to over and up to six runs (it is unusual but not impossible for a wide to fly over the boundary) to both total and runs conceded by bowler;

Bye: delivery that eludes batsman and

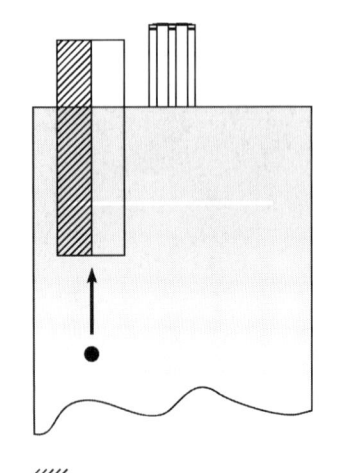

One-day wide

First-class wide

Cricket

wicketkeeper, enabling batting side to complete one or more runs;
Leg-bye: delivery that strikes the batsman's body and rebounds far enough away to enable one or more runs to be taken. If not inadvertent, no runs count. One of the sillier rules.

FIELDERS

Players entrusted with cutting off runs, making catches and effecting run outs. Arranged and assigned by a captain, usually – though not necessarily – in consultation with each bowler, in accordance with the areas in which the striker is deemed likeliest to hit the ball. The safest catchers tend to operate from the *slips*, a cordon behind the striker's wicket in which any edged strokes beyond the wicketkeeper's reach may be safely held; the pace at which the ball travels makes hand–eye coordination paramount. By and large, the swiftest runners and surest throwers patrol the *covers*, the most popular location for shots. For those whose

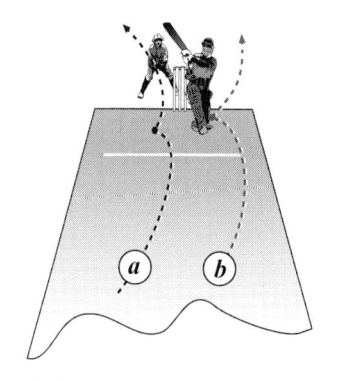

a) Bye; b) leg-bye

On the attack: four slips, short leg – typical field for new-ball bowler

only virtue is a strong arm, a spot at *fine leg*, *long leg* or *third man* is the norm: behind the wicket, near the boundary, out of harm's way. Those with the sharpest reflexes and greatest courage (and often the least seniority) can expect to find themselves stationed close to the bat at *silly point* or *short leg*. To encourage batsmen in the limited-overs format, *fielding circles*, marked in the cover and midwicket regions, are used to prevent over-defensive field settings: for the first fifteen overs of an innings, only two fielders are permitted to stand outside the circle, leaving vast unmanned expanses in the outfield (see **Playing the Field** section, p. 87).

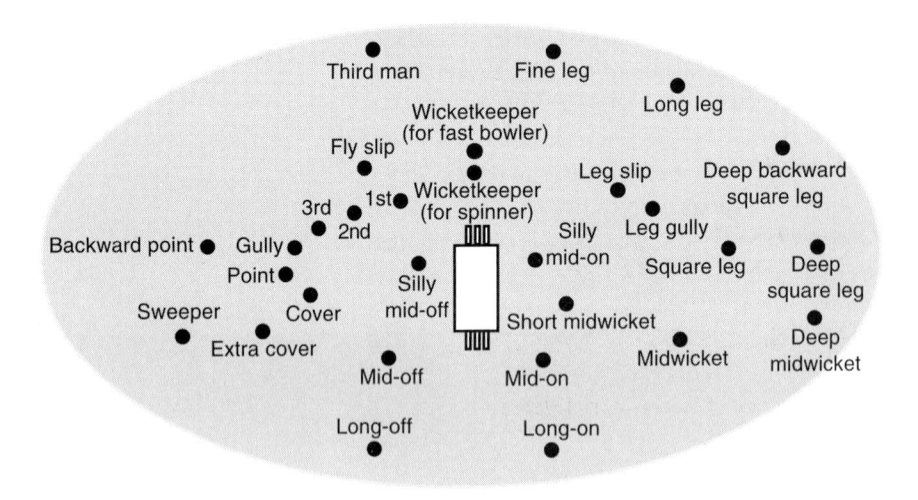

```
              Third man      Fine leg
                              Long leg
                 Wicketkeeper
              Fly slip (for fast bowler)
                                Leg slip    Deep backward
                   1st  Wicketkeeper                square leg
              3rd      (for spinner)
                   2nd              Silly   Leg gully
Backward point  Gully                    mid-on  Square leg   Deep
              Point      Silly                              square leg
       Sweeper   Cover   mid-off    Short midwicket     Deep
            Extra cover                         Midwicket  midwicket
                       Mid-off    Mid-on
                       Long-off   Long-on
```

Positions are divided into those on the leg side and those on the off:

Off side in front of wicket: mid-off (halfway back to the boundary), silly mid-off (suicidally close), silly point (squarer but still suicidal), point (square of the wicket), cover (midway between the wickets), extra cover (closer to the bowler's end), long-off (deep and straightish).

Off side behind wicket: 1st-4th slip, fly slip (deeper), gully (far end of slip cordon), backward point (just behind square), third man (just inside the boundary).
Leg side in front of wicket: mid-on, silly mid-on/silly leg, square leg (square of the wicket), deep square leg, midwicket (midway between the wickets), deep midwicket, long on.
Leg side behind wicket: leg slip, leg gully, backward/deep backward square (at an angle of 45 degrees), fine leg (at an acute angle, just inside boundary), long leg (between fine leg and deep backward square).

One position acquired from the limited-overs form has been that of the *sweeper*, a man at deep midwicket or deep cover entrusted with 'sweeping up' any shots missed by the infielders.

FIVE-FER

The bowler's century: five wickets in an innings. As in 'five for 78', or 'five-fer.'

FLANNELED FOOLS

Literary *nom de plume* for cricketers.

FOLLOW-ON

If the team batting second in a two-innings game trails by a certain number of runs (150 in first-class fixtures, 200 in Tests), the opposing captain is entitled to ask them to bat again immediately, i.e. enforce the follow-on. If he feels that the pitch is likely to deteriorate badly and hence make life difficult for the side batting last, he is equally entitled to demur. In 1961, as part of a general effort to stimulate 'brighter' play, the option was suspended in the county championship for two seasons; the benefits were not obvious. Only twice in Test history has a side won the match after following on.

Until 1900, enforcing the follow-on was mandatory, the change in the law hastened by England's failure to win the 1899 Ashes Test at Old Trafford after Australia had been obliged to follow-on but saved the game comfortably. Up to that point, the inflexibility of the rule had been roundly criticised for penalising the team in the ascendant, however inadvertently. It was also susceptible to all manner of disreputable machinations. In 1897, an Essex bowler had 'the bright idea', as Sir Derek Birley so eloquently put it in his marvellously incisive tome, *The Willow Wand*, of ensuring Lancashire made enough runs to avoid the follow-on by bowling wides to the boundary. 'The batsman, Arthur Mold, not to be balked, knocked down his own wicket.'

Appealing: Dominic Cork

GREENSWARD

Literary *nom de plume* for the field of play.

HAT-TRICK

Three wickets with successive balls.

HOWZAT

Universal imprecation 'how's that?' made by bowler and/or fielders to umpire in the hope of eliciting a favourable decision, regardless of whether or not that belief is justified. No translation necessary.

ICC

Aka International Cricket Council, the game's governing body. The nine Test-playing nations are all full members and qualify automatically for the quadrennial limited-overs World Cup; associate members, ranging from Scotland and Denmark to Gibraltar and Fiji, compete for the ICC Trophy, a junior World Cup, with the leading teams qualifying for the senior version. Founded in 1909 and based at Lord's (see **MCC**), although there are moves afoot to relocate to Calcutta, home base of Jagmohan Dalmiya, who became the ICC's first elected chairman in 1997. Formerly the Imperial Cricket Conference (and briefly the more diplomatic International Cricket Conference), the ICC had hitherto been dominated by England and Australia, the founder members, who retained a right of veto until the 1980s.

JAFFA

Unplayable delivery; 'peach' of a ball. Derivation wholly mysterious.

KNOCK

(a) Individual innings; (b) painful blow to the body, as in 'he took a knock'.

LAWS

Other sports have their rules and regulations, but cricket has its Laws, all 42 of them (plus endless riders and sub-clauses). Of these, the most asinine is indubitably that pertaining to run outs. Namely, that if a fielder's throw hits the stumps after the batsman has regained his ground, further runs may be collected from any ensuing rebound (see **Overthrows**). The fielder is thus penalised for a job well done.

MCC

The world's most famous cricket club, at once a great British institution and a source of national shame. The average age of its membership may not be quite as high as one might suppose – 57 as of 1998 – but the Marylebone Cricket Club is still seen as *prima facie* evidence of English cricket's inalienable right not to come to terms with the twentieth century.

Invariably referred to by its initials (one sceptic dubbed it the Marylebone Clodpoles Club), the precise details of its birth remain obscure. While reference works date its year of foundation as 1787 – held by historians to be the year in which Thomas Lord, a Yorkshireman working in the wine trade, established a new cricket ground in London – the club was almost certainly in existence before then.

Mecca: Lord's, the game's most hallowed venue

Cricket

Initially patronised by the likes of the Earl of Winchilsea and Colonel Lennox (later the Duke of Richmond), who advised Lord that they would support him if he laid out a private ground, the MCC has been ensconced amid the splendours of Lord's, the wine trader's third such ground, since it opened for business in St John's Wood, north London, in 1814. Oozing elegance and Empire, not to mention privilege and politesse, **Lord's** remains the game's most celebrated venue as well as the symbolic home of English cricket. If there is a more hallowed saloon bar in the land than that in the pavilion Long Room, your guide, certainly, is wholly unaware of it.

Until 1968, when it ceded power to the TCCB, the MCC ran the game in England. Contrary to widespread assumption, however, even though the club remains the custodian of the Laws, and until the late 1970s lent its name to the country's representative touring teams, and for all that Lord's still houses the major administrative offices, the MCC no longer wields much influence, at least not in any overt way. Lord's, on the other hand, still hosts a wider variety of games during the course of a summer than any major venue in any major sport; not only the professional peaks – two Tests, two Cup finals and most of Middlesex's home county championship fixtures – but the amateur awaydays (the National Village final, the National Club final). The waiting list for membership is so extensive that new applicants must trundle to the rear of a twenty-year queue. Entry is open to anyone in possession of a fully-functioning Adam's apple.

In 1998, a year after the Vienna Philharmonic had decided that women could be trusted to play Wagner without letting the side down, the MCC took a vote on whether to open its doors to the

WELL I NEVER !

In 1997, Sir Donald Bradman became the first living Australian to be commemorated on a postage stamp issued for Australia Day. One stamp featured an action shot, the other a portrait, both depicting him in his 1930s pomp.

Something in the water: Bill Woodfull, the Australian captain, regained the Ashes on his birthday in 1930 – and again four years later.

Fortune snarled at the first Pakistan women's team to venture abroad. Ignored at home by disapproving menfolk, the Karachi Ladies Cricket Club (founded 1988) left for New Zealand in January 1997, unannounced and unloved. Visa trouble en route in Singapore was followed by humiliation in the opening one-day match. Canterbury made 425 for 6, the weary travellers 44.

Losing track: Robert Vance of Wellington conceded a world-record 77 runs in one over in 1990, then prided himself on a job well done. Being the penultimate over of the game, the ruse was to keep Canterbury interested in chasing a seemingly impossible target and thereby encourage them to take risks in the final over. Vance played his part to the full, serving up 17 easy-paced no-balls: Lee Germon scored 69, including 8 sixes. So befuddled were the umpires, however, the over was called after only five legitimate balls. Requiring one run off the final ball of the contest, the Canterbury batsmen did the decent thing and didn't bother trying.

Better late than never: After 30 Tests (and 51 innings) without a century, Bobby Simpson made amends with a will in his thirty-first. Captaining Australia at Old Trafford in 1964, the opener compiled 311 in twelve and threequarter hours, the highest score ever made at the ground and the longest innings ever played against England.

Rodney Redmond (New Zealand) and Andy Ganteaume (West Indies) are among a select band of more than sixty players to have scored centuries in their maiden Tests. Neither represented his country again.

Along with le cowboy, la cover-girl and le hot dog, le cricket has been accepted by the Academie Française as part of the French language.

Jimmy Matthews, a leg-spinner from Victoria, is the only man to take two hat-tricks in a Test, against South Africa at Old Trafford in 1912. Aside from that, he had no other successes in the match. Indeed, in his remaining seven matches for Australia he took just ten wickets.

In 1962, Joseph W. Filliston umpired a match at Lord's. He was 100 years old.

Sartorial elegance made a sharp exit during the 1996–7 one-day Shell Cup competition in New Zealand. For their home games, Auckland – or, rather, the Auckland Aces, as their caps and shirts decreed – elected to wear dark blue shorts over long white socks and white bicycle tights.

According to a letter in *The Times* in 1989, a cricket league was in operation among the native women of New Caledonia in the French Pacific; men were excluded from the field of play and entrusted with the scoring. The correspondent suggested they would be worthy opponents for England.

ladies. Members had been stung into action by the refusal of a £4.9m grant by the National Lottery (one of the main reasons cited was the exclusivity of the clientele). Mind you, working out why such a sizeable slice of public funds should be donated to one of the nation's wealthiest clubs is no simple matter, even if it is 'a private club with a public function'.

The upshot was predictable: although most members, for the first time, were in favour, the requisite two-thirds majority was not attained. Despite the ground's impressive facelifts – the new Grandstand and Mound Stand are proud monuments to tasteful modernism – that prehistoric heart is still beating fast. Quite what the Queen thinks about being patron of a club that refuses to have her as a member has yet to be revealed.

'In 20 years' time', explained one staunch upholder of chauvinist piggery with some trepidation, 'the Lord's shop might be full of twin sets and lingerie in MCC colours.' Another dissenter, John Bromley, who was once refused permission to remove his jacket in the Long Room amid temperatures of 82 degrees, hit the proverbial nail on the head: 'Well, honestly, it's a gent's club. Women – I adore them. Magnificent creatures. But Lord's is my little world and I just don't want them in the Long Room.' Happily, guidelines recently issued by the Equal Opportunities Commission may soon compel Mr Bromley to usher them into his little world with open arms.

NEW BALL

Aka new cherry. Available at the start of an innings and every eighty overs (in Tests) thereafter. Being at its hardest, bounciest and shiniest, and with the seam at its proudest, the ball is then theoretically of greatest use to the fast bowlers. Not only does it travel faster, its smoothness means it is more inclined to swing. On the other hand, this may work to the batsmen's advantage. While excess swing or bounce can produce wild inaccuracy, the faster the ball comes on to the bat, the faster, logically, it comes off. When Micky Stewart became England's first team manager in 1986, he urged his fast bowlers to treat the new ball 'like a new bride'.

NIGHTWATCHMAN

If a wicket falls within twenty minutes of the end of a day's play, a non-specialist batsman may be promoted in order to forestall the loss of a more valuable wicket than his own. He may even be instructed to take as much of the bowling as possible, thus reducing the risk of an accredited partner being dismissed. The downside is that a wicket may be sacrificed needlessly.

OPENERS

The bricklayers. Strictly speaking, the term can just as easily be applied to bowlers – whichever two players are entrusted with the new ball form the opening attack – but almost invariably refers to the batsmen who commence an innings. The onus is immense. Obliged to negotiate the ball at its newest and the pitch at its freshest (in theory), they are the advance party. It is their duty to 'see the shine off' the ball, to set the tone, eschewing risk and digging foundations for the more aggressive middle-order. Geoff Boycott, England's

Top man: Geoff Boycott

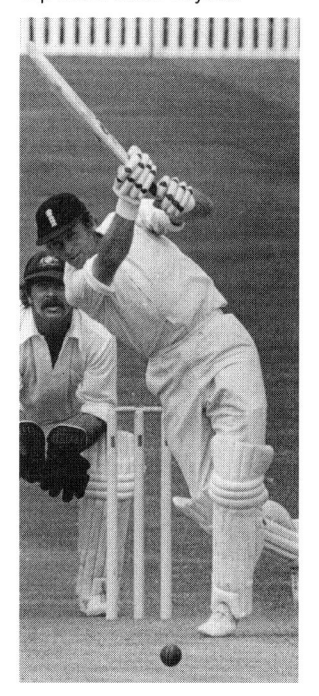

premier opener of the 1960s and 1970s, was characterised by one of his captains, Keith Fletcher, as 'the best slow batsman in the world'. At the opposite extreme was one of Boycott's many partners, the elephantine Colin Milburn, to whom defence represented the last line of attack. 'I've always been a slogger', he unabashedly declared, 'and my father was a slogger before me.'

The value of an opening stand cannot be measured purely in terms of runs: in 1998, at Port of Spain, Trinidad, England's Alec Stewart and Mike Atherton added a circumspect 129 at barely 2 runs an over, some 284 fewer than the Test-record opening liaison between India's Vinoo Mankad and Pankaj Roy (v New Zealand, 1956). More importantly, they claimed the psychological high ground, convincing their confreres that victory – now 96 runs away – was possible. And so it proved, even if seven wickets were lost in the process. It marked the first time an England team had ever scored the highest total of a Test in the fourth innings and won.

OVERTHROWS

Additional runs deriving from an errant throw. Intensely galling for the fielder, especially if he darts in to prevent a quick single, shies at the stumps, misses by a whisker and sees the ball scoot on to the boundary for a total of five. Credited, perversely, to the batsman.

PAIR

Two ducks in the same match. Two first-ball ducks constitute a 'king pair'. Aka pair of spectacles (visual impression of two 0s in the scorebook).

PITCH

Beware those who claim to be able to 'read' a pitch. They're usually bluffing. No cricketing subject, in fact, attracts quite as much unmitigated tosh.

Forget all those bumpy soccer grounds, muddy rugby fields and sodden golf greens: no other playing surface in sport can match a cricket pitch when it comes to influencing the outcome of a game. On no account to be confused with the *wicket* (unless you're Australian, that is), its character, real or imagined, determines the mental state of the protagonists. The interpretation of its likely behaviour dictates team selection and whether a captain chooses to bat or bowl first (see **Toss**). Beauty is in the eye of the winner.

'Cricket pitches are discrete creations, almost like personalities. Each one is a unique and purposefully managed amalgam of soil, grass and water.' Thus pronounced *The Oxford Companion to Australian Cricket* – and who is this mere Pom

Yorkshire bitter: Headingley, a perennial source of pitch controversies

to argue? Located in the centre of the playing area (aka the *middle*), on a *square* that, at busier grounds such as Lord's, may accommodate a dozen or more, it is watered, cut and rolled by the groundsman and his staff for months leading up to, and even during, a game. Although artificial pitches are used in schools and among the game's poorer/less grassy outposts, those used by professionals tend to be composed of clay or loam; much the heavier, the latter is part-clay, part-sand, part-decomposing vegetable matter.

Glance through a record book and a couple of things should soon become apparent. First, the pitches of the Victorian era were distinctly awkward (hence the welter of quick finishes and meagre scores); second, those of the 1930s were more like divans (hence the welter of endless matches and towering totals).

Anyone in any doubt about cricket being a batsman's game, a traditional refrain among bowlers of all persuasions, need only contemplate the reasons commonly given for lynching the groundsman (aka the *curator*). Without being too obvious about it, pitches are generally prepared to suit the home side's strengths: those perceived as offering inordinate, uneven or non-existent bounce, exceptional movement off the seam or lavish turn are condemned by hosts and visitors alike. Ditto those deemed too damp. Or dry. Anything that prevents batsmen from being beastly to bowlers. Serve up one that makes bowlers feel like Sisyphus and the only things that don't bat vigorously are eyelids.

Practical considerations, unfortunately, mean that this imbalance is likely to remain. If every five-day contest was over halfway through its designated course, the loss of income would be the death of the five-day play.

Geological factors come into play: certain venues have certain reputations for certain pitches. Until recently, the WACA in Perth, Western Australia, was a paceman's paradise: hard, fast and bouncy, as testified by the fact that batsmen edged catches behind the wicket considerably more often than they were bowled or lbw, dismissals that are often a consequence of inferior bounce. Its counterpart in Sydney, on the other hand, habitually aids spinners: ever since the square was dressed with a topsoil of new clay in 1984, the bounce has been low and the pace slow. During the late 1970s and early 1980s, the surfaces in Melbourne dried too quickly while the subsoil remained saturated, air couldn't get to the roots, bacteria set in and the grass ailed or died. The upshot was a combination of unhealthy grass and bare soil, resulting in a bumpy surface and a wayward bounce. The entire square had to be dug up and relaid.

Whacked: the WACA, Perth, the ground least loved by timid batsmen

In modern times, the most controversial square has without doubt been that at Headingley, Leeds. Granted, it may have been the stage that in 1930 saw Don Bradman achieve the unique feat of scoring 300 in a single day's play of a Test, but the decline has been steep. The shit initially hit the fan in 1961, when England thrashed Australia with more than two days to spare; so unplayable was Fred Trueman he picked up five wickets at one stage without conceding a run. 'The wicket was the colour and texture of an ant-bed tennis court', recalled the gritty Australian all-rounder, Ken Mackay. 'There was no suggestion that [it] was doctored. It was simply the result of treatment with fertiliser.' In 1972, when Derek Underwood spun England to victory over Australia inside three days, the official word was that the pitch had been infested by a little-known disease known as fuserium; the Australians were highly sceptical.

Headingley's next Ashes Test three years later brought a semblance of poetic justice: England's victory charge was foiled by activists from the 'Free George Davis' campaign, who drew attention to their cause by pouring oil over the surface, forcing the match to be abandoned. 'I'd throw them off the top of the pavilion', barked Trueman, now a radio commentator. 'Mind, I'm a fair man, I'd give them a 50–50 chance. I'd have Keith Fletcher underneath trying to catch them.'

Keith Boyce, the highly-strung Headingley groundsman, was even more livid prior to the 1985 Ashes Test. 'There's a bastard in my family', he growled helplessly, 'and it's sitting out there.' In fact, the pitch played like a dream, offering something for everyone: the bounce was true, the scoring free. There were two centuries, and seven other knocks between 46 and 91. Yet there was also pace, movement and stacks of wickets for the faster bowlers, and even a matchwinning spell from a spinner. And not until the final hour of the game did England prevail. Some bastard.

PLAYED ON

Batsman edges ball into his stumps, either because he's being overly ambitious or has been hopelessly beaten for pace. Recorded as 'bowled' rather than 'hit wicket'.

POPPING CREASE

Front edge of the batting crease, the safe haven where the batsman stands and beyond which the bowler's front foot cannot stray.

QUICKIE

Bowler of express pace. *Aka* Paceman, Pacer, Speedster, Tearaway, Horseman of the Apocalypse.

REFEREE

Off-field official – usually a notable ex-player – introduced in 1991 for Tests and one-day internationals to uphold the ICC Code of Conduct, the brief to ensure a game is played according to the spirit of the Laws as well as the letter. Responsible for judging (and implementing fines for) dissent, intimidation of the umpire, slow over rates and general conduct unbecoming (see **Crimes and Misdemeanours**). One of the more justified dissenters of recent times was Pakistan's Aamir Sohail. In a one-day international against Australia in 1997, he disputed the umpire's decision to award a catch at long leg, legitimately arguing that, under limited-overs rules, since the delivery bounced above shoulder-height, it should have been called a no ball. The referee construed this as an attempt to challenge the authority of the officials and fined him.

His Curtness: Curtly Ambrose

RETIRED/ RETIRED HURT

If a batsman willingly 'retires', usually to give another colleague a chance to bat in an inconsequential match, he is regarded as having been dismissed and may not resume his innings. If he retires hurt, either through injury or sickness, he may bat again provided at least one other wicket has fallen. During England's 1970–1 tour of Australia, Geoff Boycott, a batsman never knowingly guilty of selflessness, was forcibly 'retired' by his own colleagues after scoring a century: they were anxious to have some practice themselves.

RUNNER

Summoned when a batsman is in too much pain or discomfort to run for himself. The substitute, usually already dismissed, will stand at square leg when the batsman is on strike; when he is not on strike, the runner will take his place at the non-striker's end while the batsman retires to square leg. The potential for confusion is not inconsiderable. It is not uncommon to see a runner taking off while both batsmen dash away simultaneously from the other end.

SCOREBOARD

The outer skin of a game. Most grounds have two so that at any given moment, every non-slumbering spectator can see the score, who is batting, who is bowling, and when the last wicket fell; greater detail is available from those sold to spectators as a *scorecard* (and updated throughout the day), as well as those published in newspapers (updated daily). Listing each team in batting order (full initials and surname), these fuller boards also inform you how each man was dismissed, what the score was when

Cricket

each wicket fell, and how each bowler performed. One-dimensional and texture-free.

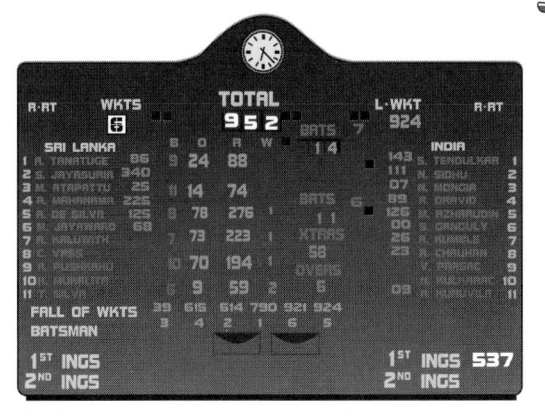

The final arbiter: the scoreboard in Colombo commemorates Sri Lanka's record Test total

a) Cut

b) Forward defensive

c) Glance

d) Backward defensive

STROKES

Various means by which a batsman collects runs or defends his stumps, played off either the *front* or *back foot*. Timing, footwork and the ability to keep the ball along the ground are far more relevant than brute force. Key adjectives: *correct, authentic, handsome, elegant, stylish, effortless, crisp, forceful, strident, boisterous, belligerent, swashbuckling, uninhibited, murderous, ugly, inelegant, stolid, sturdy* and *boring*.

Forward/backward defensive – defensive shot against good-length ball; *prod* – unambitious shot in front of wicket; *straight drive* – self-explanatory; *off-drive* – on the off side, straightish; *on-drive* – on the on side, straightish; *cover/extra-cover drive* – driven squarer; *glance* – angled fine off the legs behind the wicket; *hook* – behind wicket on leg side, ideal riposte to a bouncer; *cut/late cut* –

59

Inside the Game

e) Pull

f) Hook

g) Off-drive

behind wicket on off side, played against ball wide of off-stump; *square cut* – cut played square of the wicket; *pull* – in front of wicket on leg side, played against short delivery; *reverse pull* – batsman turns round and pulls to off side; *sweep* – square of or behind wicket on leg side, played on one knee against spinners; *reverse sweep* – batsman turns round and sweeps in opposite arc towards third man. If the ball is struck with the meat of the blade, it is said to have been *middled* (aka *clouted*, *thumped*, *larruped* or *murdered*). Less, um, cultivated strokes include the *cow shot*, *slog*, *welly*, *hoick*, *smear*, *biff*, *bash* and *wa-hoo*.

SWING

The game's greatest conundrum. Quite why a cricket ball swings is something that continues to baffle players and scientists alike. The bowler's grip is supposed to have something to do with it, humidity even more. Trouble is, the latter theory looks as if it has been well and truly demolished. Dr Brian Wilkins, a research fellow at Victoria University in Wellington, New Zealand, recently fired balls at 70mph in a variety of conditions from an adapted crossbow: by measuring the swing force on the same ball in a wind tunnel, in humidity ranging from 40 per cent to 80 per cent, he demonstrated that it made not a jot of difference.

All the same, Dr Wilkins did not contest the long-held assumption that the amount of swing varies according to climactic conditions. Using four vacuum cleaners, he believes, he has shown why. Since the crossbow pushes the ball forward, the seam or roughened side can be kept in the same position throughout its path, and thus obtain swing or even – depending on the extent to which the ball is mutilated – *reverse swing*. Adjusting the vacuum cleaners to 'blow', and connecting them to piping extending from crossbow to pitch, he drilled numerous fine holes along the top of the piping through which the air would be propelled. Dr Wilkins maintains that the resulting impact of micro-turbulence, emanating from the rise of hot air in sunny conditions, confounds the usual airflow and prevents swing; by the same token, cloud cover means no micro-turbulence and potentially enough swing to keep Benny Goodman bopping in his grave. Similarly, swing may also be liberal if the pitch is damp: the moisture keeps the grass cool and stops micro-turbulence.

Mystifying, hotly-debated and thoroughly modern, reverse swing is within the rules but subject to suspicion. The bowler will either scuff up or soak one side of the ball with sweat and/or spittle (other substances have been suspected), thus making it heavier, while shining the other. If all goes to plan, the combination of air currents and the angle at which the ball is held will turn what the bowler's grip suggests will be an inswinger into an outswinger (or vice-versa). An article in the magazine *New Scientist* seems as helpful as any:

'As a ball moves faster through the air, the sheer speed begins to cause turbulence in the laminar boundary layer, as it would even if the ball were a perfectly smooth sphere. The turbulence begins towards the middle of the ball, moving forwards as the ball's speed increases. If a ball is bowled fast enough, the boundary layer will trip into turbulence even before it reaches the seam. Now the aerodynamics are completely changed. The seam acts like a ramp, pushing the air on its side away from the ball. This makes the boundary layer

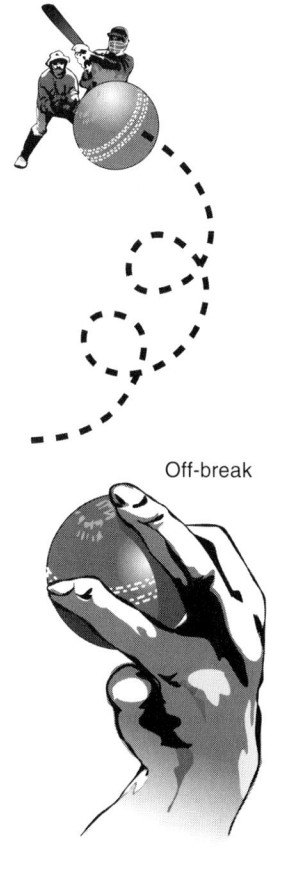

Leg-break

Off-break

thicken and separate more quickly on the seam side, which creates a side force pushing the ball in the "wrong" direction – from the seam side to the smooth side.

'A ball bowled in the conventional way needs to reach between 80 and 90 miles an hour before it will perform a reverse swing. Because few swing bowlers have ever matched [Imran] Khan's ability to reach this pace, there the matter might have rested with reverse swing remaining an oddity unique to one or two exceptionally fast bowlers. But while scientists were experimenting, so were the Pakistani bowlers. They found a trick that lowers the speed at which reverse swing takes hold. The trick is simply to allow the ball to scuff up on one side and then bowl with this side forward rather than the smooth side. The boundary layer becomes turbulent more easily on the rougher surface than it would on a smooth leading surface. This means that turbulence starts in front of the seam at a lower speed. So, with the seam still acting like a ramp to thicken the layer and cause separation, reverse swing becomes effective at a lower speed.'

Got all that?

TEA

For which everything does indeed stop. As it does for *lunch*. The latter is a forty-minute adjournment at the end of the first two-hour session of play; two hours later comes the cuppa, which lasts twenty minutes. Depending on climatic conditions, *drinks breaks* may also be taken at the end of every hour. Tea can be delayed up to half an hour if a team has lost nine of its ten wickets but flexibility is otherwise non-existent.

When lunch or tea is due, even if a side only needs one run to win, they must wait until after bellies have been properly replenished. Asked what he would do to improve the game, Phil Tufnell, the England spinner, made his priority abundantly clear: 'Longer tea-breaks.'

TOSS, THE

Arcane method, involving a coin of unspecified denomination, by which captains decide who bats first, often the most crucial element in any game. Originally used to confer choice of pitch, there was one brief period of sanity: for thirty-five years after the Laws were revised in 1774, the visiting side was entitled to choose.

Given the option, advised one expert, one should bat nine times out of ten, and on the tenth occasion ponder the alternative and still bat. Recent history, however, has undermined that theory: while the West Indies quickies were dominating the game in the 1980s, they consistently elected to field first, partly in order to extract the maximum from any early life in the pitch, but mostly to put the opposition on the back foot at the earliest possible opportunity.

'He could never make up his mind whether to call heads or tails', said Ray Illingworth of his one-time rival for the England captaincy, Colin Cowdrey, alluding to a broader capacity for dithering. Not that inspired guesswork is a guarantee of victory. Clive Lloyd, the most successful Test captain of all, called correctly less than half the time (35 out of 74) yet his West Indian XIs still won three times as many games as they lost (36 to 12). By contrast, Lindsay Hassett

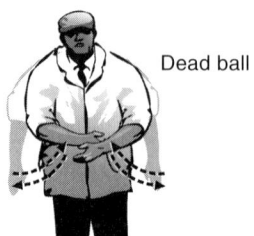

(Australia v England, 1953), the Nawab of Pataudi (India v England, 1963–4) and Garfield Sobers (West Indies v New Zealand, 1971–2) each contrived to win all five tosses in a series yet failed to gain a solitary victory on the field. Hassett, the poor lad, actually managed to lose the series.

UMPIRES

When John Snow, the England fast bowler, was asked in the High Court why he deserted the flag to join Kerry Packer's 'mercenaries', one of his reasons prompted a titter or two in the gallery. 'I have nightmares', he revealed, 'about having to become an umpire.' The job requirements are certainly daunting: excellent maths, a degree in geometry, the wisdom and impartiality of a judge, expertise in hand-signals, X-ray vision, ample reserves of stoicism and a high boredom threshold. As Bill Alley, the former Test umpire noted upon swapping white flannels for white jacket in 1969: 'It's not easy taking up umpiring when you've been an umpire baiter for over 30 years.'

Alternating positions at the end of every over, one umpire stands directly behind the bowler's stumps, the other at square leg at the other end of the pitch. The former presides over appeals against the batsmen (see **Crimes and Misdemeanours**), signals boundaries and minor offences; the latter adjudicates on line decisions (stumpings, run outs) and other infractions his partner may not be in a position to spot. If the umpire decides a batsman is out, he will raise a forefinger with due solemnity. The benefit of any doubt is supposed to go to the batsman, though the reality is increasingly at odds with this principle. During the 1997 Ashes Test at Old Trafford, John Hampshire confirmed the

Cricket

arrogance of many of his breed: 'Doubt?' he grinned. 'There's never any doubt.' One of his colleagues, the Indian Sri Venkataraghavan, was big enough to confess to being wrong at least 10 per cent of the time.

As television replays began to expose umpiring errors, so the clamour grew for TV replays to be employed to spare umpires further embarrassment and enhance accuracy. Acceptance, as ever, was slow, not least among those who feared this would undermine the umpires' sovereignty. At first, in 1992, replays were permitted for stumpings and run outs, necessitating the introduction of the *third umpire*, who monitors proceedings via a TV screen and communicates his verdict by walkie-talkie (not that he is always consulted); at that point, either a green light flashes (in) or a red one (out). Not until 1997, though, were his powers expanded: now, if there is any doubt whether a catch has been taken cleanly, technology can have the final say.

Another belated progression made this decade has been the ICC international panel, a group of independent salaried umpires employed to officiate (or *stand*) in Tests all over the world; with only one umpire from the host nation permitted on the field in such a match, charges of hometown bias have been reduced if not eliminated. The step was taken in the wake of a number of unseemly altercations, the most notorious of which saw Mike Gatting, the England captain, and Shakoor Rana, the Pakistani umpire, prod fingers at each other's expansive chest: an entire day's play was cancelled, and the match only restarted when Gatting made a written apology. A few months later he was sacked; although a different reason was cited at the time (he was reported to have celebrated his birthday in the

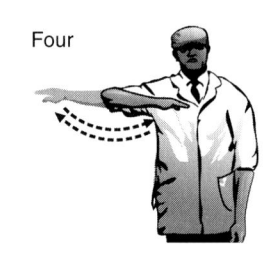

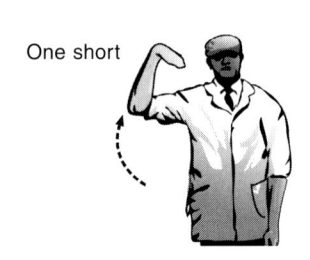

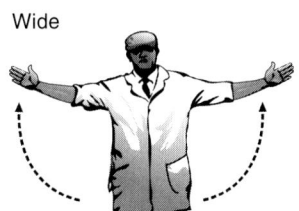

No ball

Bye

Four

One short

Wide

65

middle of a match by inviting a barmaid to his hotel room), few doubted that his show of direspect lay at the heart of it. 'The only acceptable form of dissent is a dirty look', warranted one of Rana's English counterparts. 'And we don't like that.'

George Parr, a legendary Nottinghamshire stalwart of the 1840s, had the right philosophy. 'When you play in a match', he recommended, 'be sure not to forget to pay a little attention to the umpire. First of all enquire about his health, then say what a fine player his father was, and, finally, present him with a brace of birds or rabbits. This will give you confidence, and you will probably do well.'

Signals:
Out: index finger thrust in vicinity of heavens
Four runs: side-to-side flourish with big finish
Six runs: arms aloft (waggling wrists optional)
Wide: arms at 9.15
No ball: arm at 45 degrees
Bye: arm raised
Leg-bye: one arm raised, other touching leg
One short (batsman fails to ground bat properly while running): tap shoulder
Dead ball: lower arms then cross and uncross

V, THE

As in 'he drives through the V' – area in front of the batsman (who acts as the base of the V) from mid-off to mid-on. Any batsman who does so is deemed to have been taught correctly.

WALKING

Quite simply the most honourable, magnanimous and downright honest of all sporting gestures. If a

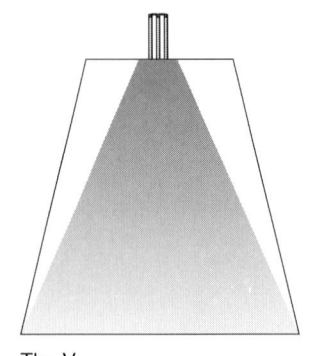

The V

batsman gets the thinnest of edges to a ball en route to the wicketkeeper's gloves, he is quite likely to be the only man on the field capable of *knowing* he hit it. In 99 per cent of cases he will await the umpire's verdict, hoping for a reprieve, but even in these increasingly pressurised times there are still those who pride themselves in doing the right thing. Sometimes, mind, this can be taken to extremes. In 1965, England's Ken Barrington staged a one-man protest against the South African batsmen's unwillingness to 'walk' by doing precisely that himself, even though he knew he wasn't out.

The practice, it should be pointed out, owed little to noble aspirations: it stemmed from English cricket's class-based roots. Not only was it a way for the batsman to assert his social superiority over the bowler, it was a means of rubbing in the fact that he also occupied a loftier pedestal than the umpire: he, not the official, was the ultimate judge. In this case, however, the means amply justify the end. There have even been instances of batsmen walking for an lbw decision. To take but one contrast, jaws dropped in horror when Robbie Fowler, the footballer, owned up to 'diving' in order to secure a penalty kick; he was even berated by the manager of the England team, Glenn Hoddle, who claims to be a born-again Christian, for betraying his team. Whenever a cricketer does something similar – fielders often own up to not completing catches cleanly – he is merely fulfilling expectations.

WEATHER

No ball game is so beholden to nature's whim. Sun, rain, snow, clouds, fog and even smog: you name it, play has halted because of it. On five occasions, the elements have been so inclement that a Test match has been abandoned without so much as a ball being bowled.

Since a damp pitch (and, to a lesser extent, a wet outfield) can have such a drastic effect on the complexion of a match, anything more than light drizzle is usually an excuse to stop play. The umpires must also consider the light 'playable', i.e. not dangerous to batsmen (the visibility of the fielders is seldom taken into account). The officials are aided by portable light meters and a column of five electric bulbs on the scoreboard, though the latter, a recent innovation, is primarily there to keep spectators informed; as a rough guide, if five bulbs are gleaming, play is unlikely to continue for much longer unless the fielding captain calls on his slow bowlers.

Weather may be the bane of the game (especially in England, where snow once stopped play in June), yet it can also add spice. Or, rather, it used to. At Melbourne in 1937, long before the introduction of full covering, heavy rain followed by blazing sunshine turned the pitch into a *sticky wicket*, i.e. virtually impossible to bat on for any length of time. Hoping to take advantage, Don Bradman closed Australia's first innings at 200 for 9, whereupon 'Gubby' Allen, his opposite number, declared England's first innings at 76 for 9, trusting that there would still be enough devil remaining to discomfit the opposition batsmen and leave his side with a reasonable target once conditions had eased. Bradman then had the bright idea of reversing his batting order, sacrificing his less adept batsmen: at 97 for 5, Australia looked to be struggling, but then Bradman and Jack Fingleton, in the unaccustomed roles of No.6 and No.7, added a record 346. Australia wound up with 564, ultimately romping home by 365 runs. They don't play 'em like that anymore.

WICKET MAIDEN

Not Lady Macbeth or Maggie Thatcher, but an over in which the bowler takes a wicket while denying any runs. If no wicket falls it is merely a maiden, accounted for in the bowler's *analysis* (or 'figures'): this is expressed as the number of overs he has bowled (O), the number of maidens (M), the number of runs conceded (R) and the number of wickets taken (W). The nearest to a 'perfect' analysis in professional annals belongs to Brian Langford: in 1969, playing in a 40-over Sunday League match against Essex at Yeovil, the Somerset spinner failed to take a wicket in his alotted eight overs but then nor (more importantly in the context of a one-day game) did he concede a run. The entry against his name on the scorecard read 8–8–0–0.

WOMEN

For all that a woman invented overarm bowling and the England women's team have won two World Cups to their male counterparts' none, cricket has always treated them as second-class citizens (see **MCC**), in Britain at least. Not until 1976 were they invited to adorn Lord's; even though female spectators were allowed into the pavilion on the day of the match, they had to be accompanied by a member. In Australia, the leading players are respected professionals; until 1997, their counterparts in England were still forking out for their own kit. Enlightenment, happily, is beginning to peek through. In 1998, the Women's Cricket Association was invited to amalgamate with the England and Wales Cricket

Women: grudging acceptance

Board, a reflection of the growing interest among young women: the 1997 season saw 1,910 matches involving 167 women's clubs and 96 male clubs with women's sections. At school level, there were 456,000 active players.

XENOPHON, CONSTANTINE BALASKAS

Lavishly-monikered leg-spinner of Greek descent whose nine wickets at Lord's in 1935 earned South Africa their first Test victory in England. Aka 'Saxophone'.

YIPS

Sudden, incomprehensible loss of form and mechanics, especially among left-arm spinners; akin to stage fright. Research at the Chelsea School of Physical Education in London suggests that sufferers find they can bowl quite proficiently until they are being watched.

ZZZZ

Reaction of the uninitiated or uneducated. 'Say', wondered Groucho Marx, turning to his neighbour halfway through a match on his first and last trip to Lord's. 'When do they begin?'

HOW _____ Cricket

PLAYING THE GAME

'Cricket is full of theorists who can ruin your game in no time.'

Thus declaimed Ian Botham, one of the more instinctive talents ever to grace a field of play. Here, nevertheless, are some pointers from the experts:

Don Bradman (Batting)

'Bradman was the summing up of the Efficient Age', attested Sir Neville Cardus, that most colourful and lauded of cricket writers. 'Here was brilliance safe and sure, streamlined and without impulse.' Bradman's biographer, Charles Williams, the MP and former Essex player, begged to differ. Here he analyses the importance of grip and stance to the game's greatest phenomenon:

'His technique was wholly his own. He was as far removed from orthodoxy as it was possible to be. He had, after all, taught himself, with a stump and golf ball; and such was the speed of his reactions that he never felt the need for coaching into a more traditionally acceptable style.

'No more than five feet eight inches tall, with small shoulders, but with long, powerful arms and wrists which could clamp on to a bat handle like a vice, he had a method which was almost impossible to imitate. To begin with, he held his bat in what for anyone else would have been an uncomfortable position. Instead of the handle running across the palm of the right hand and resting against the ball of the right thumb, with the left wrist in front of or to the side of the handle, he twisted his right hand round so that the handle pressed directly against the ball of the right thumb while his left was turned round so that the wrist lay almost behind the handle.

'Furthermore, he rested his bat on the ground before delivery, between his feet rather than behind his right foot, as is usual, and made no movement (except during the "Bodyline" series) until the bowler was committed to a particular length of ball. From this there followed two natural results: first, that his bat was lifted at an angle of almost 45 degrees from the line of trajectory of the ball; and, second, that if the chosen stroke was across the line of the ball rather than directed straight back down the wicket his instinctive movement was to roll his wrists over in making the stroke.

'It was this second movement that made him such a powerful player on the leg side, particularly in his favourite shots – a push wide of mid-on and – almost his trademark – the pull to midwicket from a ball short of a length just on or outside off stump, and that made him such a master of the late cut through the slips.

'For anybody else, of course, it would have been impossible with such a grip to hit the ball with any force in the arc between mid-off and cover point. Bradman's off-drive, however, was one of his fiercest shots, achieved by exercising – with exact timing – the full power of his formidable right wrist at the point of impact with the ball. What was impossible for anybody else was a lethal weapon for Bradman.'

(Adapted from *Bradman* by Charles Williams, Little, Brown & Company, 1996)

Bradman's most productive shot was the pull.

The Don: Donald Bradman

Here he describes his approach:

'When I was very young and just beginning to learn the rudiments, I was compelled to play most of my cricket on concrete pitches covered with coir matting. These pitches give rise to a more uniform but much higher bounce than turf. I was very short and found great difficulty in playing with a straight bat the ball pitched short of a length. It came too high for comfort. To overcome this, I developed the pull shot to a marked degree.

'It simply consisted of going back and across with the right foot and pulling the ball with a horizontal bat somewhere between mid-on and square leg. Because of my grip I was able to roll the wrists over as the stroke was played and keep the ball on the ground. Keen eyesight was needed.

'Turf is much more uncertain than concrete and after arriving in Sydney I began to lose my wicket occasionally because the greater speed and lower bounce of the ball off the turf sometimes caused me to hit over the ball and be bowled or lbw. When that happened the shot looked a real haymaker and I am sure this, above anything else, gave rise to the story that I played with a cross bat [bat swinging across the line of the ball instead of through it]. Actually, there is no other way to play the pull shot, but on turf greater judgement is required and the stroke must be used more sparingly.

'No batsman should attempt to pull a ball which is over-pitched or of good length. This is courting disaster. However, assuming the ball to be the right sort, the method is very similar to the hook. Go back and across with the right foot so that the right toe is pointing almost straight down the pitch towards the bowler. Then as the ball comes along (normally knee to stomach high) pull it hard to mid-wicket – at the same time pivoting the body and rolling the wrists over to keep the ball on the ground. In many respects the movement is similar to the square cut, but instead of cutting against the line of flight, you pull with it. In order to control the shot and to have the best chance of combating any uneven bounce, it is essential to pivot the body and get the legs fairly well apart. At the finish the batsman should find himself facing square leg.

'I was counselled by many older players to give the shot up. They said it was too risky. But I was loath to do so because I felt sure it would bring me lots of runs.'

(Adapted from *The Art of Cricket*, Hodder & Stoughton, 1958)

Prince Ranjitsinjhi (The late cut)

No stroke can match the late cut for elegance or eloquence. In addition to being the first batsman to defend on the back foot, Kumar Shri (Prince) Ranjitsinhji was held by all who saw him to cut later and more felicitously than anyone. His exceptional reactions helped him attain the highest career average (56.37) by any county cricketer scoring 10,000 or more runs.

'The late cut is made by putting the right foot identically in the same place as for the square cut (in a line with the off stump). But the ball is hit later – that is to say, when it has passed the batsman's body, and very often after it has passed the wicket. It is made with a quick, sharp flick of the wrists. A player with weak wrists should not attempt the stroke. The secret is a power to use the wrists.

'The bat should hit the ball, and not the ball the bat. Though the shot is effected almost altogether by the wrists, still, by letting the body bend from the hip so that it follows the arms and hands in the direction the ball is played, more power can be imparted. Like all other strokes, the cut should be followed through as far as possible.

'Accurate timing is facilitated by putting the leg across before the stroke is actually made, so that in making the stroke the player is standing firmly on both legs. Accuracy of aim is much increased by a firm stance. When a player is moving about at the time of making a stroke, his actual aim cannot be so sure as it might be. And accuracy of aim is very essential for good cutting.'

(Adapted from *The Jubilee Book of Cricket*, Blackwood, 1897)

Brian Lara (Batting out of a slump)

In May 1994, the one-man Posse from Trinidad was the most fêted figure in the game. He had just set new records for the highest innings in first-class and Test cricket (501 not out and 375), yet insisted that he had learned solely 'from watching the great players in action – I've never read a coaching book in my life.' Anti-climax, inevitably, was swift, and he struggled through the first three Tests in England the following year, his highest score after five innings a disconcertingly mortal 54.

'I was really panicking. I wanted to know what was happening. Was I going to let the season pass without getting the runs? Dominic Cork kept

Feline: Brian Lara

getting me dead in front (lbw). I'm the sort of player who never studies technique. If I get a fault I try to get rid of it immediately. Cork used to run so close to the wicket that I needed to open up [my stance] and wait a little longer before I made my decision to play.'

(From the *Daily Telegraph*, May 1996)

NB: Lara's last five innings in the series yielded 87, 145, 152, 20 and 179.

Fred Trueman (Fast bowling)

In 1964, Fred Trueman of Yorkshire and England, the self-styled 'greatest ruddy fast bowler that ever drew breath', became the first man to take 300 Test wickets. Asked whether he could envisage anyone matching him, the retort was typically theatrical: 'Whoever does will be bloody tired.' Frank Tyson, a former Test colleague, a renowned purveyor of pace himself, paid tribute:

'Physically he hardly seemed destined for athletic greatness. He was no Greek statue, but the truncated breadth of his characteristically square fast bowler's frame was lined with an even strength from shoulder to hip. His feet, those ploughmen of many a batsman's wicket, like those of most great athletes, turned in and imparted their bent to his pillared legs. Even the square lines of his jaw bespoke a certain pugnacity and power.

'But there was nothing incongruous about his bowling. His parabolic approach from the regions of a straightish mid-off was rhythmically smooth, and stridingly long. Only the portly advance of years curtailed the long circular swing of his classically erect left guiding arm. His action was faultless in

Bullish: Fred Trueman

its body-swing, his bare-chested, sparsely-haired chest affording the sensibilities of mid-on and his metalled right toe braking the pent-up power of his troublesome final seven-league stride until the last volcanic moment.

'His delivery, like that of his hearty fellow tradesman Ray Lindwall, was perfectly suited to out-swing, on which most of his effectiveness was based. Even the Australian pitches, enervating on man and ball alike, could not curb his movement to the slips. His very first ball there, in 1958, resulted in West Australian batsman Jack Rutherford being caught in the slips. Even when he bowled a standard length, he elicited disproportionate bounce from the pitch; it was just as if he hit it as hard as he would have liked to strike the batsman.

'Outwardly at least, he assumed the mantle of greatness with complete self-assurance. He was the Cassius Clay of fast bowling and whilst he did not always state that he was the greatest, one always felt that his mastery was founded on this confidence. I suppose that deep down he was motivated by that unreasoning, mad-cap, fast-bowling force – the earnest desire to bowl really quick. In his declining years he still considered himself just as fast as on that day in Hull in 1949 when I saw him for the first time, a raw 18-year-old. But the very prop of his cricketing existence was his unswerving allegiance to Yorkshire.'

(Adapted from *Great Bowlers* by Frank Tyson, Pelham, 1968)

Dennis Lillee (Bouncers)

Lillee formed one half of the most lethal new-

Demonic: Dennis Lillee

ball alliance in the game's history; his partner, Jeff Thomson, once declared that nothing thrilled him more than the sight of a pitch spattered with a batsman's blood. Mike Brearley admired Lillee, in particular, and saw him as rather more than a sadistic bully-boy:

'When Lillee writes, "I bowl bouncers for one reason, and that is to hit the batsman and thus intimidate him", he tells a fraction of the truth. For he clearly has other reasons for bowling bouncers, as well as the one he owns [up] to. He often hopes, in the first place, to get the batsman out with a bouncer, whether mishooking or defending. And, secondly, he intends to force the batsman to change his technique; to be wary of pushing forward to him, for example. Good bouncers are unsettling technically as well as psychologically.

'I agree with Lillee in so far as he is saying *one* reason for bowling [bouncers] is to intimidate. Physical courage, allied to skill, plays a part in many games and sports ... At Perth, in 1979, I think that some of our [England's] batsmen were secretly unnerved by an image of Australian toughness. We lost contact with our own combative powers and surrendered to the legend of Lillee and the Perth pitch. (I remember that Botham was so angry about his tentativeness that he batted with a kind of reckless fury himself – yet another inappropriate reaction.)

'Mastery in cricket can be achieved by all manner of means, and a side's need to muster all its grit, cunning, patience and team spirit is even more crucial when it lacks the edge in sheer power.'

(Adapted from *The Art of Captaincy* by Mike Brearley, Hodder & Stoughton, 1985)

Angus Fraser and Curtly Ambrose (Seam bowling)

In seeking to discover the effectiveness of his own attack, the England coach, David Lloyd, took meticulous note of every single delivery bowled in the third Test at Port of Spain, Trinidad, in 1998. Going a considerable way beyond the call of duty, he also categorised each delivery in terms of length, line and type. Dispatching this information to a computer researcher at Lord's, he obtained the following results for the teams' respective spearheads, Fraser (England) and Ambrose (West Indies):

Fraser
LINE: 44% just outside off-stump, 21% on off-stump, 11% wide of off, 14% on middle, 7% on leg, 3% just outside leg.

Since Fraser was aiming for the area from just outside off-stump to middle stump, in the hope of hitting the stumps or eliciting an edge, he can be said to have been 79 per cent successful.

LENGTH: 62% good, 18% full, 14% marginally short, 1% short, 5% half-volley.

Since he was aiming between good and full, 80 per cent successful.

TYPE: 72% straight, 20% off-cutter, 5% leg-cutter, 1% inswing, 1% outswing, 1% slower.

Consistency, rather than variation, is the key.

Ambrose
LINE: 35% just outside off-stump, 25% on off,

11% wide of off, 13% on middle, 10% on leg, 6% outside leg.

Like Fraser, he concentrated his focus around off-stump and middle, and was 84 per cent successful.

LENGTH: 52% good, 17% full, 22% marginally short, 4% short, 3% bouncer, 2% half-volley.

Since he was aiming between good and full, and the bouncers were intentional, 72 per cent successful.

TYPE: 59% straight, 32% off-cutter, 8% leg-cutter, 1% inswing.

More consistently varied than Fraser: nearly half his deliveries were off-cutters or leg-cutters.

In the case of both men, the dearth of swing (a combined 1.5 per cent) emphasised the degree to which the bowlers felt that the pitch, rather than the atmospheric conditions, would assist them. Their belief was not misplaced: Ambrose claimed 8 wickets for 87, Fraser, the winner of the man of the match award, 9 for 90. England won.

Shane Warne (Spin bowling)

At Old Trafford in 1993, Shane Warne dismissed Mike Gatting with his very first ball in an Ashes Test, a delivery universally acclaimed as 'The Ball of The Century'. Pitching outside leg stump, it spun back almost two feet, darted behind the batsman's legs and struck the top of off-stump. Warne's recollections also encompass a delivery in the same match which he considered superior:

'The call comes: "Warnie, you're on next over".

A few loosening swings of the shoulders and a few stretches of the arm and fingers. It takes me about an over and a half to really feel loose, but for some reason I've always been able to land my first few balls fairly accurately. Some spinners start with a few innocuous deliveries just to get into a rhythm. I usually start with my stock ball, the leg-break, and I usually try to spin it a fair way. As it left my hand it felt just about perfect.

'When a leg-break works really well it curves away to the leg-side in the air before pitching and spinning back the other way. The curve in the air comes from the amount of spin on the ball and in this case I had managed to put quite a lot of purchase on this delivery. That is why it dipped and curved away so far and then spun back such a long way. I knew I'd bowled Gatt and I could tell from the look on Ian Healy's face behind the stumps that the ball had done something special, but it was not until I saw a replay during the lunch break that I fully realised just how much it had done. After stumps the England players came into our dressing-room for a drink and Gatt just looked up at me and said, "Bloody hell, Warnie. What happened?" I didn't have much of an answer for him. "Sorry mate. Bad luck." Then we both laughed.

'It came from nowhere – a great thrill but not quite as satisfying as setting up a good batsman, working a tactic out to counter his technique then bowling the right ball. That is what happened in the second innings. Alec Stewart had been pushing forward to me but keeping his hand close and sometimes half behind his front pad. The leg-break was turning so he refused to follow it ... I also tried wrong 'uns and toppies but Alec was able to cover them with his pads as well.

'So what to do? The zooter is one ball I bowl that not many people understand. Basically, it looks like a leg-break when it leaves the hand, but the difference is that it floats out of the front of the fingers with some backspin on it. The batsman expects [it] to turn but instead it often floats through to him fairly harmlessly and then goes straight on off the pitch. It sometimes dies on pitching too, whereas the top spinner, which also usually goes straight through, tends to dip in the air and jump off the pitch. The zooter tends not to do much at all ...

'The plan with Alec was to continue giving him leg-breaks and let him keep letting them go, then to slip in a zooter and hope that he doesn't pick it or that it was not spinning sideways through the air like a leggie. In that case the ball might just take the edge of the bat on the way through. It pitched on a length just outside off stump, Alec pushed forward again and kept his bat in close to his knee expecting another leg-break to spin past. But the zooter kept its line, clipped the edge and Healy took a wonderful low catch. It might have looked like a nothing ball but that was exactly what it was supposed to look like.'

(Adapted from *My Own Story* by Shane Warne, Bookman, 1997)

Alan Knott (Wicketkeeping)

Renowned as much for his constant exercising as for the speed and athleticism of his glovework, Alan Knott was as fit as any player who ever trod a greensward. The 1970–1 Ashes series may have marked his finest hour, but he began the tour with a severe knee problem:

'I was desperate not to lose mobility, otherwise I would lose much of the technical requirement for a wicketkeeper. As it was I was handicapped by my lack of hamstring mobility.

'A wicketkeeper needs to be able to take the ball with legs as straight as is comfortable in order to have the correct "giving" room – in other words, so that he can bring his hands back a very similar distance every time, at whatever height the ball may be. My hamstrings meant that I had to bend my knees, and the "giving" room available was therefore dependent on the height at which the ball was taken. I would rather not have had to do as many exercises as I have done, but they have been essential for me. You see people gliding around like ballet dancers and I would love to have been like that. Instead I find that at least half an hour's stretching exercise is necessary every morning when I get out of bed.'

Knott's mentor and inspiration was Godfrey Evans, his larger-than-life predecessor for Kent and England, whose (then) Test record of 219 dismissals he ultimately eclipsed:

'His energy, strength and enthusiasm made a real impact on me. Watching Godfrey "live" for the first time in 1965 made me wonder how great he must have been at his peak. He had the patience to wait for his chance to come yet he looked to attack every ball, especially for stumpings, and he displayed an aggressive attitude in diving full length to catch or take. He was prepared to go for anything. That was one of the most important lessons he taught me – never hesitate.

'He would encourage continually, keep you going, particularly if things went wrong. You might drop the easiest catch of your career but off the next ball you could take one of your best. He was always living for the next ball, for the next moment in life.'

(Adapted from *It's Knott Cricket* by Alan Knott, Macmillan, 1985)

Ian Chappell (Captaincy)

Ian Chappell captained Australia thirty times between 1971 and 1975, winning fifteen Tests and losing just five. In seven series, he won five and drew two. 'Playing against a team with Ian Chappell as captain', observed Mike Brearley, another esteemed leader, 'turns a match into gang warfare.' Here 'Chappelli' evinces a more thoughtful side:

'Australia's great old leg-spinner Bill "Tiger" O'Reilly used to write that a well-trained collie dog could captain a cricket team. While I share Tiger's implied admiration for man's best friend, I didn't entirely agree with his pet theory. Certainly a collie could arrange a batting order, manipulate the bowling changes and direct fieldsmen. However, they are only a minor part of the tasks.

'A skipper must be prepared to plant some seeds (by spending time with his players after hours) if he wants to reap rewards on the field and become a respected leader. Once he's acquired that status he's well on the way to becoming a good captain. Respect is vital. He must earn it in three categories: as a player, as a human being and finally as a leader. If he achieves those aims and complements them with a good knowledge of the game which he applies with common sense and a dash of daring and he's endowed with a reasonable share of luck, he's on the way to a rating of excellent. If he also

Gang warfare: Ian Chappell

has very good players around him, then there's no stopping the guy.

'There is one sure way to get the best out of a team: make the cricket interesting. A captain shouldn't fear losing, but he should hate losing. There's a big difference. The former will be defensive, the latter aggressive. Why? Because in the first case he will do everything to avoid defeat, including manoeuvring into a position from which he can't lose before he goes for the win. The second type will go flat out for victory from ball one and only opt for the draw when all hope of winning is lost.

'Richie Benaud and Les Favell, both excellent attacking captains, had different ways of achieving the same result. Richie, a bowler, expected his team to bowl as many overs in a day as possible: the more balls delivered, the more opportunities to take wickets. Les, an opening batsman, demanded that South Australia make 300 in a day's play, reasoning that scoring quickly allowed the bowlers more time to take wickets. If we batted first and were 320 for 7 at stumps, "Favelli" was as happy as a new parent, but if we were 280 for 2, he was like an Indian on the warpath.

'A good captain must be observant and have a good memory. Listen, watch and file things away: you never know when they might bring about the downfall of an opponent. One certain way to gain respect is to ensure the game is played in a manner that is hard but fair. Any captain who condones cheating will quickly lose respect. He shouldn't expect an invitation to every player's birthday party; it's not a popularity contest. Good captaincy is about leadership. Most players want to be led. That's why a collie wouldn't make a top-class captain – they're always the one attached to the lead.'

(Adapted from *The Oxford Companion to Australian Cricket*, Oxford University Press, 1997)

Don Bradman (On selection)

'What is the ideal makeup up of a Test match team? What type of players, in other words, would you select to achieve the perfect balance of batting and bowling strengths under normal playing conditions?

'Two recognised opening batsmen of whom one shall be a left-hander; three other batsmen of whom one at least should be a left-hander; one all-rounder; one wicketkeeper who is also a good bat; one fast bowler to open with the wind; one fast or medium pace to open into the wind; one right-hand off-spinner; one left-hand orthodox first-finger spinner.

'England's team at the Oval in 1956 went very close. She had a left- and right-hander to open, but there was neither a left-hand batsman nor an all-rounder in the next four. The Australian team of 1921 also went very close. There was not a left-handed batsman from two to six, but as Jack Gregory [one of two all-rounders, batted at No. 7] was left-handed he partially made up for this. Two fast bowlers opened, Gregory and McDonald. Then, instead of my theoretical off-spinner and left-hand spinner, the team had Warwick Armstrong, a nagging, persistent type of slow leg-spinner with a genuine googly bowler, Arthur Mailey, to complete the side.'

(Adapted from *The Art of Cricket*, Hodder & Stoughton, 1958)

Cricket

PLAYING THE FIELD

To help explain the whys and wherefores of setting a field, here are three responses to particular match situations.

1) England v Australia, Third Test, Headingley, 1981: Bob Willis to Dennis Lillee

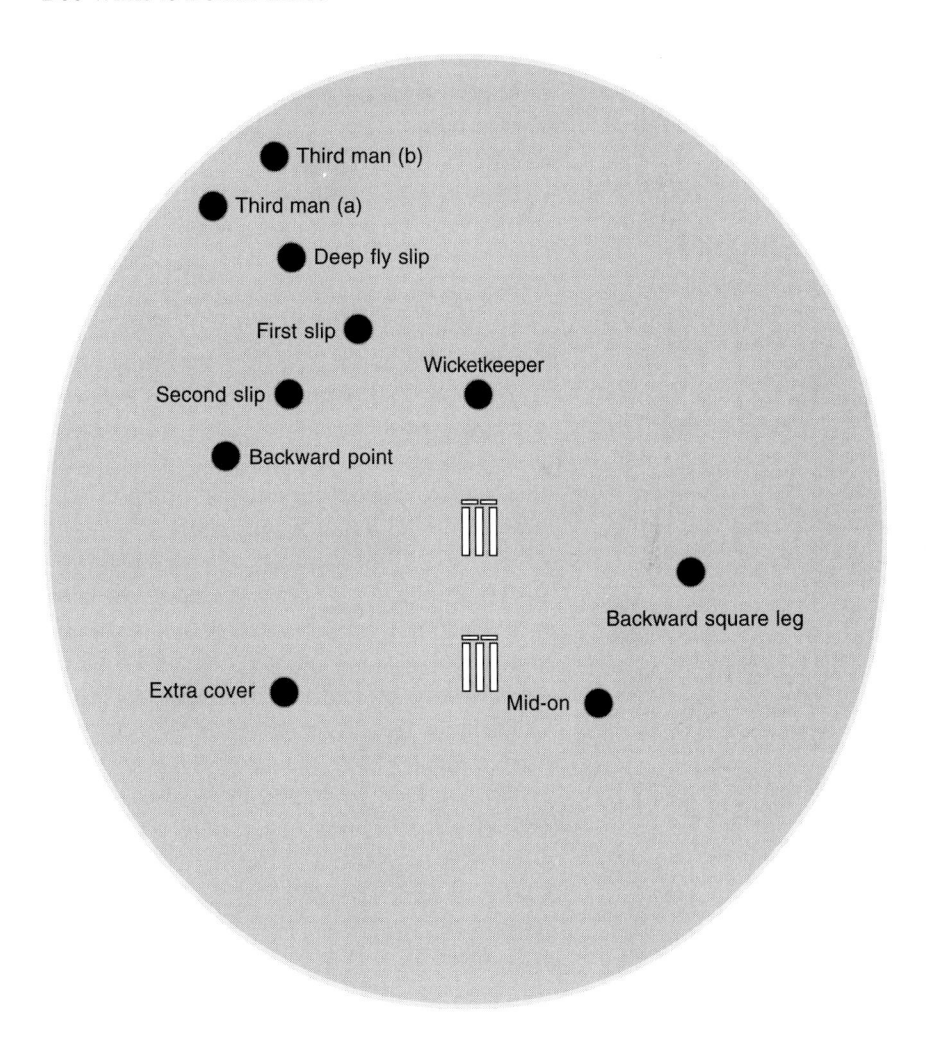

87

WELL I NEVER!

Impostors: a Julius Caesar played for Surrey, a William Shakespeare for Worcestershire and a George Bernard Shaw for Glamorgan.

Farook that: Angered by a decision, Farook Mohammed beat an umpire unconscious with his bat in Winnipeg, Canada. He was acquitted of attempted murder but found guilty of aggravated assault and possession of a dangerous weapon.

Shattered dreams: A fund-raising match at Twyford, Bristol, in 1989, made a total of £44, £1 less than the club had to fork out to replace a window smashed during the course of the day by a six.

Wrong way round: George Coulthard umpired in a Test before he made his debut as a player. He stood at Melbourne in 1878–9 – where he saw Fred 'The Demon' Spofforth take the first Test hat-trick – and was picked to play at Sydney three winters later. Quite why is uncertain. He batted at No.11, didn't bowl and never won favour again. The following year he died of consumption.

Two former Indian Test players, Jasu Patel and R.H. Shodhan, went on hunger strike in 1989 until the deputy Mayor of Ahmedabad consented to consider their plea: that matches of importance should be played at the city's renovated Sardar Patel stadium.

Marvellous Marvan: against New Zealand at Dunedin in 1997, Marvan Atapattu, the Sri Lankan batsman, improved his Test average by 2182 per cent in half an hour. Having made just one run in his previous six innings – including two pairs – he scored 25 to swell his average from 0.17 to the giddy heights of 3.71. Another 22 in the second innings spirited him to the nosebleed territory of 6.00.

Oxford University's G.E.V. Crutchley retired on 99 not out in the 1912 Varsity Match at Lord's owing to a dose of measles.

In 1991, the year the Laws of the game were first translated into Chinese and Japanese, Australian and British troops did their bit to spread the gospel with an impromptu 'Test' in Northern Iraq. After the Australians had won, the equipment was distributed among the bewildered Kurds.

Upholding the Trades Descriptions Act: Lahore's Real Twelve Brothers CC lives up to its name with a vengeance, featuring a dozen members of the Sarwar family ranging in age from 36 to 16. Ashraf, the eldest, manages the team and plays only if one of the others is unavailable.

Dean Jones was 160 not out and in a bad way. Dehydrated in the merciless 40-degree heat of Madras in 1986, fresh from spending the previous night in hospital on a saline drip, the Australian batsman was vomiting between balls. 'Mate,' he said, turning to his partner, captain Allan Border, 'I've had enough. I can't move my arms, I've just pissed in my pants and I'm in a mess.' OK, replied Border matter-of-factly, 'we'll get somebody tough out here – a Queenslander.' Queensland's Greg Ritchie was next man in but Jones had no intention of having his manhood slighted any further. Girding what was left of his loins, he added 50 more, returning to the pavilion a stone lighter than he had left it. Coach Bobby Simpson made no bones about it: 'No one has ever been asked for more on a cricket field.'

Inside the Game

In the following chapter I give a blow-by-blow account of one of the most unforgettable matches in the game's history: the Third Test between England and Australia at Headingley in 1981.

At the height of the dramatics the man least deserving of envy was Mike Brearley. With Australia set a small target for victory, the England captain had to maintain the most delicate of balances between attack and defence. Bearing this in mind, he not only had to place his fielders with a suitable degree of clairvoyance, taking into account each batsman's shots of preference as well as the predilections of his bowlers, he also had to be flexible.

When Lillee steps back to poke a bouncer from Willis for a vital four, over the captain's own head at first slip, Brearley decides to take Graham Gooch from third slip and post him at deep fly slip, a seldom-occupied position twenty yards or so behind second slip, the intent to intercept any similar mis-hits. Since Lillee and his partner, Ray Bright, are scoring at will, Brearley feels he can only afford to have two men in close-catching positions – both of which should be slips, to catch edged drives or indeterminate prods – and dispatches short leg to backward square leg, saving the single. Aware of Lillee's fondness for the cut, he also takes the unorthodox step of stationing two 'third men' to patrol the boundary behind the wicket on the off side. Finding his most productive avenues blocked, Lillee adopts a more conventional approach, confining anything risky to the open spaces on the leg side. He is caught mistiming one such drive to mid-on.

Next man in is Terry Alderman, the rabbit's rabbit. Brearley consults the bowler, Botham. 'We agreed that we needed a mid-off, as Alderman's forward lunge might give him runs in this direction', recalled Brearley. 'We also needed a square leg, rather than a short-leg, to cut off thick edges or nudges on the leg side.' Which left three close fielders. Brearley wanted two slips, with one man wider and straighter at gully; Botham is adamant that there should be three. Brearley is nervous, wary that this would enlarge the gap behind cover, rendering the off side too vulnerable, but he relents. In the ensuing over, two sharp chances fly directly to Chris Old, the man occupying that very position. He drops both.

2) West Indies v England, Third Test, Port of Spain, 1998: Curtly Ambrose to Dean Headley

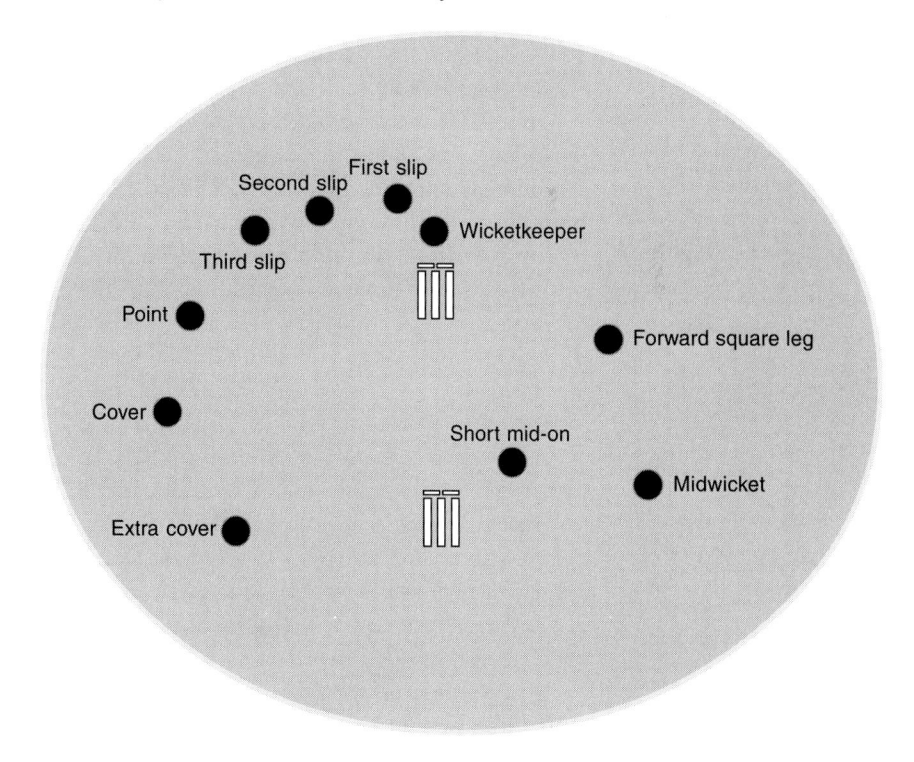

Inside the Game

Compared with Brian Lara, Brearley had it easy. When Headley and Mark Butcher return to the crease after lunch on the final day, England, with three wickets standing, need a further seven runs to reach their target of 225, whereupon a single from Butcher and a three to Headley cut the requirement to three. As they pray for their gods to spare them the ordeal of confronting Courtney Walsh and Ambrose on this enigmatic, often spiteful pitch, England's last two batsmen, Angus Fraser and Phil Tufnell, feel only marginally less queasy. Mike Atherton, the England captain, and his fellow opener, Alec Stewart, still sit side-by-side at the back of the players' area, faces grim and devoid of blood.

With Headley, a fast bowler and modest batsman, on strike at the start of Ambrose's next over, Lara knows he has to go all-out, but he can only afford to have three slips; under normal circumstances he might have deployed a fourth, and certainly a gully and a short leg. The rest of the fielders are arranged in a ring, saving the single. Seeking insurance against any wild throws, the captain also brings in mid-on to a position next to the stumps.

Offering a dead bat to the first ball, hence reducing its pace, Headley pushes gently to leg, too gently for square leg to get there in time to prevent a scampered run. Butcher on strike and the slips withdraw. Stopping runs is the prime objective now: if Ambrose can keep Butcher quiet for the remainder of the over, Walsh can have another dart at Headley. Whereupon a no ball and a leg-side bye render the fielders entirely redundant.

3) Australia v England, Second Test, Melbourne, 1994: Shane Warne to Devon Malcolm

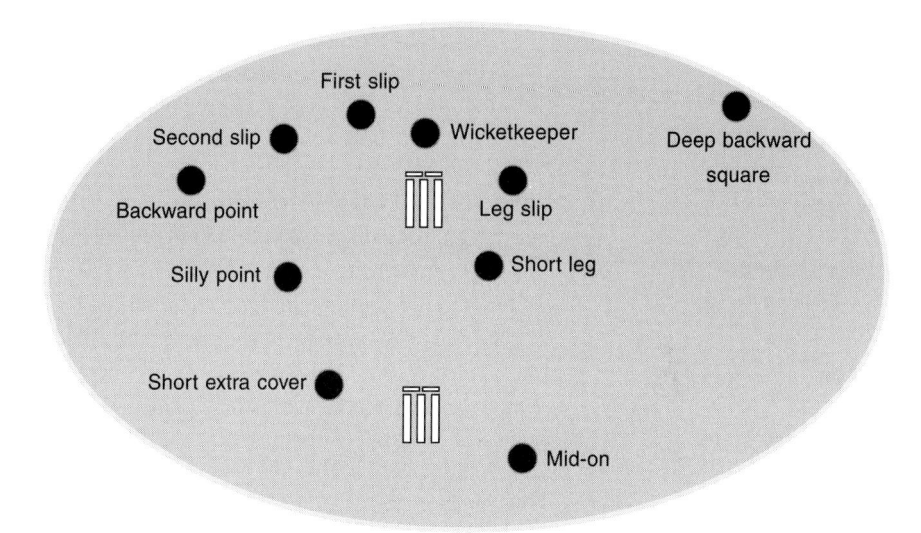

[Field diagram: First slip, Second slip, Wicketkeeper, Deep backward square, Backward point, Leg slip, Silly point, Short leg, Short extra cover, Mid-on]

Second only to taking ten wickets in an innings, the bowler's holy grail is the hat-trick: in more than 5,000 Test innings to March 1998, only twenty men had achieved it, and two of those, Courtney Walsh and Merv Hughes, spread theirs over two innings. On his home ground at Melbourne in the final week of 1994, Warne became the first wrist spinner to join this select band. It was, as he readily confessed, 'a mixture of [the] planned and unplanned'.

Pursuing an unlikely target of 388 on a pitch responsive to spin, England are already up a creek and paddle-free when Phil DeFreitas is adjudged lbw, going back to a delivery that scurries through and fails to turn as much as expected: 91 for 7. Darren Gough follows next ball, pushing forward and edging one that turns sharply and lifts for wicketkeeper Ian Healy to take a brilliant, instinctive catch: 91 for 8. Next man in is Malcolm, a fast bowler first and last. 'Devon either slogs or blocks', Warne would reflect, 'so I thought I'd bowl a big over-spinner which would either spin a little either way or go straight through.'

With the vast majority of his deliveries spinning from leg to off, shots against Warne tend to end up on the off side, hence the absence of a man at midwicket and the general dearth of fielders on the leg side. The idea behind this is to tempt the batsman into aiming for the untenanted areas, which in turn obliges him to hit against the spin, thus heightening the chances of an ensuing edge. Normally he has a mid-off and a short fine leg, halfway between the stumps and the boundary, both to save runs, but with Australia in such a formidable position such considerations are irrelevant.

For Malcolm, Warne augments his customary close-catching cordon with an additional conventional slip as well as a leg slip (it is a measure of his success in this area that Mark Taylor, his regular first slip, has taken more catches off him than wicketkeeper Ian Healy). In the first innings he had brought off a notable coup, posting Steve Waugh about twenty yards behind the wicket on the leg side; lo and behold, Mike Gatting, a keen sweeper, had mis-hit one such stroke precisely as intended and lofted the ball straight to Waugh. With Malcolm almost certain to try to block, a shallower leg slip makes more sense.

When Warne finally delivers, Malcolm prods at a ball that hurries straight through, bounces more than anticipated, clips his left glove and lobs to the right of short leg. David Boon, stationed there for exactly that outcome, belies his portly frame by diving full-length and grasping the ball an instant before it falls to earth. Mission impeccably accomplished.

_____ Cricket

THE GREAT MATCH

DAY FOUR
Headingley, 20 July 1981

'Botham's Magnificent Innings Brings England back to Life' (Daily Telegraph)

'Our only real hope of escaping from the match was if the weather came to our aid.' Thus confessed Ian Botham, mirroring the defeatist mood in the England camp. 'Our spirits were so low', reinforced Mike Gatting, 'the only consolation we could think of was that this couldn't go on much longer.' Which is why they and their confreres had checked out of their hotel.

At the outset of the fourth day of the third Test against Australia, the home team were on the brink of going 2–0 down in the six-match series. Only once in more than a century of Test cricket had a team followed on and won, and that was in 1894. Only once in that span had a team recovered from a 2–0 deficit to win a series. The Ashes were as good as gone.

'We arrived with all our kit', said Gatting, 'ready, we thought, to leave around lunchtime.' At 3 p.m., with England 135 for 7, 92 runs short of saving an overwhelming innings defeat, the new electronic scoreboard displayed the latest odds from Ladbrokes: 500–1. Roughly the same as those on a bonafide UFO sighting. Colleagues had to dissuade Dennis Lillee and Rodney Marsh, two of the Australians' more inveterate gamblers, from taking £50 out of the team kitty and putting it on the

95

opposition. Mike Brearley, the England captain, had showered, changed and packed. 'Diplomatically', noted Botham, 'he chose to put on a clean cricket shirt so that if anyone looked up at the balcony, his defeatism would not be too obvious.'

Botham greeted the new batsman, Graham Dilley, the tall, blond, young fast bowler from Kent whose claims to solid batsmanship were distinctly tenuous. Dilley grinned the grin of a man with nothing left to lose. 'Let's give it some humpty', he urged. Seldom one to need coaxing in such matters, Botham obliged, though not before Dilley had set the pace, scoring 22 of the next 27 runs.

'The Aussies found it all very amusing', smiled Botham. 'As far as they were concerned the match was all but over, the Ashes were in the bag and they could stand a bit of light entertainment from a number nine batsman they were convinced barely knew which end to pick up. But Picca [Dilley] just kept on hitting so I decided to join in. Suddenly, we had edged close to, level with, and then unbelievably, ahead of the Aussies. We were still not really in the game but at least we had given them a run for their money and the punters who stayed had something to smile about.'

Never knowingly lacking in bravado, Botham had disdained a helmet. By his own admission, he was 'playing by pure instinct' – and it showed. Hooking, pulling or cutting at anything the vaguest bit short of a good length, driving ferociously at anything pitched up – thus virtually ensuring that any edges would be uncatchable by human flesh – he was the first to concede it was 'sheer unadulterated slogging'. One inside edge flew past square leg; Ray Bright dropped a difficult catch in the gully when he had made 32. Most of his shots, though, were middled, and beefily. 'No need to look for that one', Richie Benaud informed BBC TV viewers after one savage blow off Terry Alderman. 'It's gone straight into the confectionery stall ... and out again.' Small wonder the bowlers began to get testy. Geoff Lawson lost his cool entirely, firing two beamers at Botham. For the first time in the match, the Australians were not in complete control.

Every run was cheered to the rafters, every boundary a cue for hosannas. Chris 'Chilly' Old, the next man in, looked on from the dressing-room with mounting disbelief. Brearley issued his instructions: go out there, Chilly, and play your own game – i.e. hammer everything. It was a courageous, positive decision.

Dilley perished as he had prospered, bowled for 56 swinging at Alderman after the pair had piled on 117 in 18 overs of rampant hell-for-leathering, 7 short of the record for England's eighth wicket in an Ashes Test (by Hendren and Larwood in 1928–9). Yet still the mayhem continued. Suitably emboldened, Old chipped in with a vital 29 to help Botham add a further 67 for the ninth wicket, taking the lead close to 100.

Untouched by nerves and firmly in hyperdrive, Botham hurtled through the nineties, his century arriving off 87 balls,

Inside the Game

one of the swiftest in Test history. In going from 39 to 103 he had barely had to leave his crease: thwacking and whumphing for all he was worth, 62 of those 64 runs had come in boundaries. When he had made 109, Marsh soared high but couldn't hold a mishook, the stroke executed with eyes firmly shut. It was most definitely not art, nor terribly scientific. Botham was the smithy, smiting the toffs on the village green, surfing on a wave of adrenalin, twanging his braces between balls. Come evening, he could not recall essaying a single shot in defence.

By then he was unbeaten on 145, his best in Tests: Mars the Joybringer had been restored to Olympus. All of which made it exceedingly tricky for euphoric Englishmen to confront the reality of the situation. With an entire day left and just one wicket intact, the lead was a mere 124. Good thing Lillee gave the Australian team bus driver a tenner of his own to make that wager ...

Score at end of play: Australia 401 for 9 declared; England 174 and 351 for 9.

Great but late: Ian Botham's century seemed merely to have delayed the inevitable

WHY _____ Cricket

THE BEAUTY AND THE BEASTLY

In the summer of 1997, Wasantha Kumara committed suicide. Harangued by his mother for not seeking work and devoting too much time to cricket, the 20-year-old Sri Lankan requested that he be buried alongside his bat and ball. In the hope that he might prove a better player next time around.

Wasantha was not alone in his obsession. Over five continents, aspiring batsmen, bowlers and wicketkeepers dream of playing for their country: Australasia, Asia, Africa, the Americas and Europe. To succeed requires skill, stamina and dedication, but also self-control, selflessness and a bottomless well of patience. The Laws, conventions and spirit of the game are also touted as models for socially acceptable behaviour. Cheats seldom prosper (at least not for long); loss of temper is usually fatal. If somebody hoodwinks or defrauds you, you don't stamp your foot and hiss 'it's not golf' or 'it's not tiddlywinks'. You say 'it's not cricket'.

Rewind to Melbourne, 1961, to the fifth and final Test between Australia and West Indies, to one of the game's most gripping finishes. The hosts, chasing 258 to win the series, need 4 more runs as their stout-hearted wicketkeeper, Wally Grout, faces up to an off-break from the impossibly skinny Lance Gibbs. Grout chops the delivery fine, towards the sightscreen, and runs two. As he does so, Alexander, the West Indies wicketkeeper, points excitedly: a bail is lying on the ground at the striker's end, at the base of the off-stump. In playing the shot, had Grout inadvertently knocked it off? The umpires conferred: not out. In the next over, Grout surrendered his wicket. Bemused as he was, he felt it was the right thing to do. (There was even a happy ending: his side still won.)

1300
First English reference to cricket (in wardrobe accounts of Edward I)

1550c
Game at the Free School, Guildford, Surrey; Duke family of Penshurst, Kent, manufacture their first cricket ball

1595
G. Florio's Italian–English dictionary mentions cricket

1622
Six parishioners prosecuted at Boxgrove, Kent, for playing in the churchyard on a Sunday

1676
First mention of game played overseas – by English residents of Aleppo, Syria

1694
Half a crown paid for a 'Wagger' (sic) on a match at Lewes, Sussex

1706
First full description of a match – in a Latin poem by William Goldwin (Eton & Cambridge)

Inside the Game

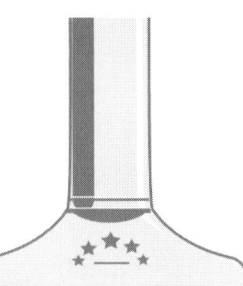

1709
First county match – Kent v London; William Byrd plays with friends in Virginia

1710
First mention of game at Cambridge University

1729
Date of earliest surviving bat, inscribed 'JC' (John Chitty)

1744
First known issue of the Laws, drawn up by the London Club (president Frederick Louis, Prince of Wales, father of George III); first recorded admission charge – tuppence to the Artillery Ground, London

1767
Hambledon Cricket Club (CC) formed

1787
Marylebone CC (MCC) forms and redrafts Laws; first mention of a county club – Oxfordshire

Ah, chorus those of a certain age, but that was then. There was less filthy lucre about, the sponsored car hadn't been invented, and the game was vastly more chivalrous. Fast forward to Port of Spain, Trinidad, 1998. During the climax of the third Test, with England scenting victory but fast running out of wickets, Courtney Walsh, the West Indies' veteran fast bowler, had an opportunity to sneak an advantage. As he ran in, he noticed that Dean Headley, the non-striker, was backing up rather too enthusiastically: all he had to do was stop in his delivery stride, whip the bails off and Headley would be run out. It wouldn't have been cricket but it would have been damn useful. Instead, he let gallantry get in the way. This time there was no happy ending.

Pele may have been the most gifted man ever to strike a ball but he was horribly wide of the mark when he dubbed football 'the beautiful game'. What, with all those brutish tackles and shameless play-actors? If any sport warrants such an accolade, cricket does. The graceful arc of bat, the teasing parabola of ball, the white-clad knights jousting honourably on sunlit pastures. To have witnessed David Gower dismiss an opposing bowler's best ball from his presence with minimal effort and optimum timing, or Bishen Bedi languidly curve his arm over and outwit a batsman with stealth and spin, is to recall a visit to a higher plane. Or, at the very least, a refreshingly unusual one.

Cricket exists in its own twilight zone. The clunk of leather on willow, sending ripples of genteel applause around village greens, is celebrated as the soundtrack to a more innocent age. In a world full of push and rush, cricket offers calm and balm, celebrating the clock rather than defying it. No sport, certainly, allows spectators to dwell on its

Cricket

charms at such length. With games lasting up to five days (a series of Test matches can go on for four months), the pace is leisurely, the propensity for abrupt plot-twists and protracted dramatics correspondingly enhanced. If a football match is pure Spielberg, all noise and speed and black-and-white emotions, a cricket match is a week's worth of Coronation Streets: the story may not unravel that far in a single episode, but you still tune in religiously for fear of missing something crucial.

Cricket is physical chess, a tussle between minds rather than bodies. Any number of lofty claims have been made about its right to be considered an art. Let's just call it the most refined and rewarding of the competitive arts and crafts.

While cricket may not have been a purely Anglo-Saxon invention – there is evidence to suggest it could well have been exported from France by soldiers in the thirteenth century – there is every reason to believe that it evolved on the Weald, where Kent, Sussex and Surrey intersect. It certainly owes its popularity to English missionaries. Genteel, conservative and wary of emotion, it is regarded as the quintessential English game. 'The game of cricket, philosophically considered, is a standing panegyric on the English character', attested the Reverend James Pycroft in *The Cricket Field*, the first history of the game, published in 1851. 'None but an orderly and sensible race would so amuse themselves ... It calls into requisition all the cardinal virtues.'

Nor is it any coincidence that the game should find its most ardent devotees in what was once the British Empire. Robert Mugabe, the first prime minister of Zimbabwe, summed up the appeal of this enduring symbolism: 'Cricket? It civilises people and creates

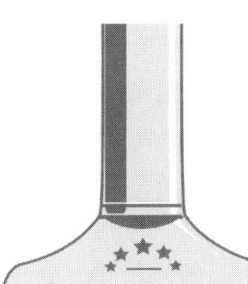

1792
Calcutta CC formed

1805
Lord Byron in Harrow XI beaten by Eton at Lord's

1806
Inaugural meeting of St Anne's CC, Barbados

1808
Match in Cape Town advertised for $1,000 per side

1825
First mention of England's 'champion county'

1827
First Oxford–Cambridge match

1841
Duke of Wellington orders every military barracks to install a cricket ground

1846
William Clarke's 'All-England XI' embarks on first national tour

1849
First Yorkshire–Lancashire match

Inside the Game

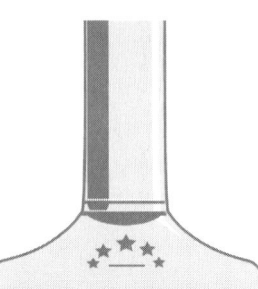

1859
First overseas tour by an English team – to US and Canada

1861
First visit by English team to Australia – major matches described by Australian press as 'Test Matches'

1864
First county championship table published; first English tour to New Zealand; 'overhand' bowling legalised; launch of *Wisden Cricketers' Almanack*

1868
First Australian tour to England

1877
First 'official' Test match: Australia v England in Melbourne

1878
First 'official' tour of England by Australia

1886
West Indies team tours US and Canada

good gentlemen. I want everyone to play cricket in Zimbabwe. I want ours to be a nation of gentlemen.'

Cricket has certainly achieved more for society than most sports. It binds the Commonwealth together, bridges racial divides. No other arena unites black, brown and white on such a comparatively level playing field. The English county championship was a multinational brotherhood decades before the Football League finally consented to imported manpower.

Then there was the D'Oliveira Affair. At the Oval in 1968, England beat Australia thanks in no small measure to a century and a vital wicket from Basil D'Oliveira, a Cape Coloured who had left Cape Town to seek his fortune (not to mention more humane treatment). A few days later, D'Oliveira was called up as an eleventh hour replacement to tour his homeland, prompting an outraged response from the South African government, under whose apartheid laws national teams were obliged to be all-white. To put it mildly, he was not welcome. 'It's not the MCC team', denounced the prime minister, John Vorster. 'It is the team of the anti-apartheid movement.'

The selectors – whose mysterious decision to omit D'Oliveira from the original party was characterised by one illustrious ex-captain as 'a good honest piece of bungling by good honest men' – refused to back down; the tour was cancelled and South Africa ultimately expelled from official international cricket until the demise of apartheid.

'Few of those within the world of first-class cricket are political animals', acknowledged John Arlott, the eminent journalist and broadcaster who had helped D'Oliveira when he first came to England (upon arriving in South Africa some years before,

Cricket

Arlott had made his views abundantly clear by filling in the 'race' section of the visa form with the words 'human being'). 'That, however, is no excuse for being politically unconscious.' The game had taken a stand (rugby union's British Lions, it will be noted, carried on visiting the republic). Its role in the downfall of the twentieth century's most abhorrent regime is not to be sniffed at.

But enough of images. With the beauty, inevitably, comes the beastly. Solidarity over South Africa was far from rock-solid (intriguingly, many of the Englishmen who breached ICC rules and the Gleneagles Agreement by playing there in the 1980s now occupy positions of high authority). Matches have been interrupted and even ended by riots. It can be a fierce, often violent game. Imagine being the target for an undersized cannonball and you will get a picture of what it is like to be a batsman (or, for that matter, a close fielder).

Frederick Louis, Prince of Wales, heir to George II, died following a blow on the head from a ball. At Auckland in 1975, Ewan Chatfield, the New Zealand seam bowler, was struck on the temple by a bouncer from England's Peter Lever. His heart stopped for several seconds before some mouth-to-mouth resuscitation from Bernard Thomas, the England physiotherapist, saved his life. Shattered jaws, fractured fingers and broken ribs are commonplace. Nor is the game free of moral dubiousness. Once, with New Zealand requiring six to win from the last delivery of a limited-overs international, Australia's Trevor Chappell, instructed by his captain and brother, Greg, rolled the ball along the ground, making the shot impossible.

The man who did most to popularise cricket, and

1889
South Africa play inaugural Test (v England); Currie Cup first-class competition launched in South Africa; first English tour to India

1892
Sheffield Shield first-class competition launched in Australia

1894
New Zealand Cricket Council established

1899
First England Test team chosen by national selectors

1900
First West Indian tour of England

1905
Australian Board of Control established

1909
Imperial Cricket Conference (ICC) formed – founder members England, Australia and South Africa

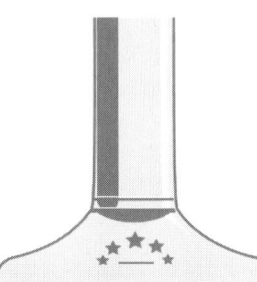

1926
India, New Zealand and West Indies join ICC; Women's Cricket Association formed

1928
West Indies play inaugural Test (v England)

1930
England's home 'Ashes' Tests extended from three to four days; New Zealand play inaugural Test (v England)

1932
India play inaugural Test (v England)

1933
Australia threaten to withdraw from Commonwealth in wake of 'Bodyline'

1938
Lord's Test televised for first time

1939
Last 'timeless' Test (i.e. played to a finish) – with England due to sail home from South Africa, match left drawn after ten days

hence turn it into England's national summer pastime, was Dr William Gilbert 'WG' Grace, the bearded colossus whose astonishing all-round feats and charismatic aura made him sport's first bonafide superstar. One admirer insisted he was 'too clever to cheat'; those who played alongside and against him knew better. To them, he was a scruple-free opportunist with no little expertise in intimidating umpires and upsetting opponents.

One of his favourite gambits was to persuade a batsman to glance up into the sun at some non-existent birds and then try to sneak the ball past him while his eyes were still dazzled. Playing against Australia, he noticed that S.P. Jones had left his crease for a spot of 'gardening' – patting down a divot in the pitch – whereupon 'the Good Doctor' urged the wicketkeeper to knock the batsman's bails off and promptly beseeched the umpire, Bob Thoms, to give Jones out. Thoms, recalled Jones's teammate, Joe Darling, 'asked Grace if he wanted a decision and on Grace saying "Yes", replied: "It is not cricket but I must give the batsman out".'

It is worth knowing that WG was still getting up to his tricks in the so-called Golden Age. 'The game had grown up', vouchsafed David Frith in *The Pageant of Cricket*, referring to the 'Roaring Nineties'. 'There was a County Championship, suitably financed, thanks to low wage bills, moderate costs, large attendances and generous private patronage. Club cricket thrived, and in 1890 the North-East Lancashire League was formed. The four-ball over had given way to five (six in Australia), and umpires began to look the part in their white coats ... cricket was being case-hardened for the 20th century as a national obsession, a pastime/industry of unshakeable importance.

The most golden of ages was about to unfold.'

That said, although the onset of a new century found standards (of batsmanship, naturally) held to be at an all-time, untouchable high, the English did not always deport themselves as well as they might. 'It must always be regretted', concluded a letter in the *Melbourne Age* during the 1897–8 MCC tour, 'that the English captain on his departure from Australia will leave a very general impression that he is a better winner than a loser.' The 'Whingeing Pom' had been born.

Not that Grace was the first to disgrace the game's avowed good name. 'Cricket is unalloyed by love of lucre and mean jealousies', declaimed Lord Frederick Beauclerk during a speech at the Thatched House Tavern in 1838. The 'sole reward', his Lordship added, came from 'the approbation and applause of the spectators'. A trifle rich, that, coming as it did from cricket's original villain.

A direct descendant of Charles II and Nell Gwynn, born in 1773, Beauclerk had progressed rapidly since leaving Cambridge University, establishing himself as the outstanding amateur batsman of the day at the age of twenty-five before rising to the presidency of the recently-formed Marylebone Cricket Club, then the game's supreme authority. Foul of mouth, short of fuse and unencumbered by fair-mindedness, he was uniformly despised. Even Daniel Dawson, a nefarious low-life who would later be hanged for horse-poisoning, declined to share a carriage with him.

By his own reckoning, Beauclerk made 600 guineas a year from gambling on matches (cricket's original public function); it was a jolly

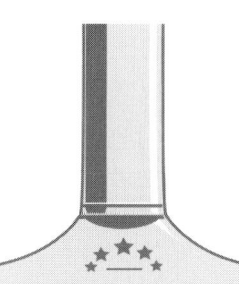

1947
First drawn Test in Australia since 1881–2

1948
Tests in England extended to five days; first tour of Pakistan by first-class touring team (West Indies)

1952
Pakistan admitted to ICC; play inaugural Test (v India)

1956
First televised matches in Australia

1963
Distinction between Gentlemen (amateurs) and Players (professionals) in county cricket abolished; first limited-overs knockout competition

1968
England tour of South Africa cancelled when apartheid government refuses to admit Basil D'Oliveira, a Cape Coloured

Inside the Game

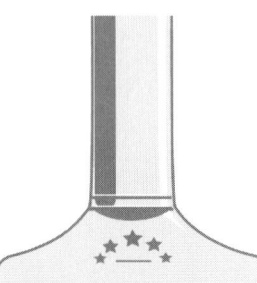

1971
South Africa banned from Test circuit; England play Australia in inaugural one-day international

1973
Bookmakers granted right to operate on English grounds

1975
First World Cup final (at Lord's)

1977
Kerry Packer signs fifty-one players for his 'circus'

1982
Sri Lanka play inaugural Test (v England)

1992
Zimbabwe play inaugural Test (v India); South Africa readmitted

1997
TV replays permitted for ascertaining legitimacy of catches; Bangladesh granted one-day international status; ICC earmarks ten countries for advancement, including Scotland, Ireland, Holland and Denmark

good thing, averred one contemporary commentator, that the MCC's sphere of influence was then rather limited, since his Lordship was renowned for stooping to any depths to ensure he won his wagers. Once, after being beaten in a single-wicket match, he asked the press not to publish the details.

He also did his best to stop the game from becoming an even contest. At the turn of the nineteenth century, underarm bowling was still *de rigeur*, yet Beauclerk and his fellow batsmen had mastered it to such an extent that even the 1798 decision to widen the wicket from 6 to 7 inches (it had already been heightened from 22 inches to 24) did little to correct the imbalance. Then, playing for Kent against All England in 1807, John Willes brought his arm up to his shoulder, reviving a form of bowling – round-arm – expressly forbidden by the MCC. (He picked it up, or so the story goes, from his sister Christina, whose voluminous crinoline skirt rendered it quite impossible for her to bowl to him in the orthodox manner.)

The umpires turned a blind eye, and persisted in doing so as the new style spread throughout Kent, but when Willes organised his county's inaugural annual fixture against the MCC in 1822, his first trip to Lord's proved to be his last. Beauclerk, the MCC captain, instructed the umpire to stop Willes from persisting with his 'illegal' action, whereupon (or so the story goes) Willes threw the ball down, leapt on his horse and rode away, never to be seen in a major match again. The cause was taken up by another Kent bowler, George Knight, a nephew of Jane Austen; eventually, in 1835, the offence was decriminalised. Sense and Sensibility 1, Pride and Prejudice 0.

THE GREAT MATCH

DAY ONE
Headingley, 16 July 1981

'Dyson Celebrates after England let Chance Slip' (Daily Telegraph)

The Midas touch has not returned, but maybe we were expecting too much. Fond indeed had been the hope that the reinstatement as captain of that wise old bird Brearley would conjure a change in fortune for the nation's benighted hero, relieving Botham's shoulders of the millstone that had reduced the world's outstanding cricketer to a careworn caricature. That Australia reached 203 for 3 owed much to 3 dropped catches, 2 by Botham and the other off his bowling. Which rather suggested that Brearley's wand was in urgent need of oiling.

Upon winning the toss, Kim Hughes, Australia's captain, made eyebrows arch violently by taking the unusual precaution of re-inspecting the pitch. Not that you could blame him for procrastinating. The clouds hung heavy, the pitch looked dry and cracked, and England's decision to omit John Emburey, their sole specialist spinner, appeared misguided. Yet when Hughes opted to bat – reasoning, presumably, that the pitch could only deteriorate, and would hence aid his own spinner, Bright – the ball moved liberally both off the seam and through the air.

But for Botham's faux pas the outcome of a rain-interrupted day might have been altogether different. The principal sufferers, though, were the crowd, whose efforts to rouse their side lacked nothing in patriotic fervour. When your team has failed to win any of its previous eleven games, depths never before plumbed by an England team, it requires a special kind of faith not to lose heart at such mishaps.

Granted, his brashness can get up the more precious of nostrils, but surely only the stoniest of hearts could fail to feel for Botham. Hailed as a latterday Biggles, the fastest swashbuckler in the west lost much of his devil during that ill-starred reign as captain, a role to which his instinctive approach had always seemed utterly at odds. With no experience of any substance, learning the ropes against the marauding West Indian pace hordes was a trial even Hercules would have blanched at.

Then, last Tuesday, came the nadir. There the woebegone lad was on that yawn-filled final afternoon at the Lord's Test, the MCC members sending him to Coventry as he trudged past them, trailing his second duck of the game. Not only were they disassociating themselves from this unrefined upstart, they were silently rejoicing in his hopelessness. Was this his reward for having his children teased at school? So he resigned; convinced that the burden of leadership had impaired his form, the selectors had planned to sack him later that day anyway.

You would have thought the fates might have deigned to give the chap a break, but no. Lo and behold, with the third ball of

Cricket

his sole over of an abbreviated morning session, he trapped Graeme Wood lbw, but this turned out to be little more than a tease. The chance he missed off Trevor Chappell cost England 59 runs; even less forgivably, John Dyson, the implacable schoolteacher from New South Wales who opened the innings boasting a Test-best of 53, had made barely half of his eventual 102 when Botham downed him in the gully: two-handed to his left, a foregone conclusion for the Superman of yore. To counter the recall of the Amazing Dancing Brears, one can only assume Hughes phoned Harrods and placed an order for some top-grade green kryptonite.

The smithy smites: Ian Botham blows away his frustrations, admired by Rod Marsh

RECORDS

There are lies, damned lies and statistics – and then there are cricket statistics. With the arguable exception of baseball, no sport is quite as helplessly besotted with numbers, and certainly none so in thrall to the decimal point. Comparatively few, nevertheless, have the substance to match their weightiness.

Take Brian Lara's record first-class score of 501, achieved in a county championship match comprising two innings in four days and destined for a draw midway through the third. Then there was that run orgy between South Africa and England at Durban in 1939, which produced the highest such aggregate in any Test (1,981) and the highest fourth-innings total in first-class history (England's 654 for 5). The match ended on the tenth day, and then only because England, who were forty-two runs short of victory, were in danger of missing the boat home.

The way the game has developed also prompts a certain healthy scepticism. Take the late George Lohmann, who established the Test record for wickets taken at the least cost (series *and* career) more than a century ago. Helpfully, he plied his trade at a time when pitches, left uncovered during the hours of play, strongly favoured bowlers: in the first 50 Test matches (1877–96) there were 96 completed innings of under 200; in nos 150–200 (1923–31) there were just 22; in nos 951–1,000 (1983–5) there were 30. Lohmann's *pièce de resistance* came in 1895–6, when he took 35 wickets in 3 matches against South Africa at an average cost of 5.80 runs, but then what sort of opposition was he facing? So hopeless were the South Africans when they joined the Test fraternity (in the winter of 1888–9), not one batsman reached 50 in the team's first 12 innings (to the end of that 1895–6 series); on Lohmann's tour they managed only one *partnership* of 50.

With pitches now protected from the elements, it was perhaps faintly inevitable that Sri Lanka should have done the unthinkable in 1997, amassing a score of 952 against India to outstrip England's 903, a Test peak that had stood for almost 60 years. Granted, only one team had mustered as many as 700 since 1958 (Pakistan 708 v England at the Oval in 1987), yet much of the gloss is removed, once again, by the wider perspective: fourteen wickets fell during the course of those five days in Colombo, an average of roughly one every two hours. When the balance between bat and ball is so utterly distorted, even the miraculous is rendered pointless.

Then there are the anomalies. The first Test between West Indies and England at Sabina Park, Jamaica, in 1998, was abandoned in unprecedented fashion when, after less than an hour's play on the opening morning, the umpires and referee agreed that the pitch was too dangerous for the batsmen. Nevertheless, because the game began, the caps awarded to the participants stand, as do the scores.

At the same time, there are the Untouchables, the landmarks that continue to amaze and confound. Among the tallest and proudest of these are Jim Laker's nineteen Australian wickets at Old Trafford in 1956, the only instance – endurance feats apart – of an individual setting an extant first-class record of significance in a Test. Still more remarkable, though, was the fate of his partner in spin for Surrey and England, Tony Lock, who bowled one more over in that match yet took 1800 per cent fewer wickets. Then there's Don Bradman's phenomenal Test batting average of 99.94; his nearest rival, South Africa's Graeme Pollock, managed 60.97.

To obtain some idea of the gulf between them, consider this: to match the Australian maestro's superiority, Michael Johnson, the world's fastest runner, would have to run the 200 metres in less than 12 seconds, i.e. 60 per cent faster than he has ever done. Sometimes, just sometimes, even cricket statistics are on nodding terms with the truth.

A TOUCH OF CLASS

THE Beauclerk–Willes divide reflected the way their sport mirrored the English class system (the professional game isn't known as 'first-class' cricket for nothing). Batting was for the nobility, bowling for oiks; bowlers served, batsmen gorged. Both the MCC and Hambledon, the game's first all-powerful club, were founded and run by aristocrats. Much loved as it was in the villages of the south, cricket derived its prestige from being fostered and nurtured at the Varsities and public schools.

The annual tussles between the leading fee-paying emporia were social occasions first and last, and none more so than those between Eton and Harrow, which drew crowds of 15,000 to Lord's in Victorian times and beyond (the admission price was inflated to dissuade outsiders). Between 1871 and 1887, almost 400,000 people attended the 'Varsity' match between Oxford and Cambridge at Lord's, an annual fixture to this day. At Fenner's and the Parks, where the universities still play, the pitches have always been prepared for the batsmen's benefit; among the scores of graduates who have gone on to play for England, precious few have been bowlers.

As county clubs formed and professionalism spread, so the divisions became ever more rigid. If you drew a wage from playing – and only oiks did that – you were a 'Player'; if you played as an amateur – and only ex-public schoolboys and social climbers could afford to do that – you changed in a separate dressing-room, entered the field via a separate gate, claimed extensive 'expenses' and were known as a 'Gentleman'. If your name was W.G. Grace, you could lead a tour to Australia, sail first-class while your colleagues slummed it in the cheap berths,

---

MAJOR RECORDS
(Men unless otherwise stated; year given where possible, or season; correct to June 1998)

TEAMS

Biggest win
First-class: Innings and 851 runs (Railways v Dera Ismail Khan, 1964)
Test: Innings and 579 runs (England v Australia, 1938)

Highest total
First-class: 1,107 (Victoria v New South Wales, 1926)
Test: 952 for 6 declared (Sri Lanka v India, 1997)
Women: 567 (Tarana v Rockley, 1896)
Test: 525 (Australia v India, 1984)

demand ten times more money than the so-called pros, and still be classified as a 'Gentleman'.

Breeding was also a passport to high office. Of the MCC's 111 Presidents between 1825 and 1939, no fewer than 95 were peers or knights. The dominant figure in the first quarter of the twentieth century was Lord Harris, the MCC treasurer and former Governor of Bombay who claimed that his entire life 'pivoted on Lord's'. For the next twenty-five years or so the reins lay with Sir Pelham Warner, son of the Attorney-General of Trinidad, educated at Rugby and Oxford, sometime captain of England and 'as deeply English', noted Richard Holt in *Sport and the British*, 'as Bertie Wooster' (with whose creator, the cricket-mad P.G. Wodehouse, Warner shared the nickname of 'Plum'). Warner donned a top hat to attend the Varsity match, and insisted on addressing professionals by their surname.

And woe betide those who dared to mess with the natural order. A spectator at the Oval in 1924 was taken aback to see Percy Fender, the Surrey captain, 'lead the "gentleman" members of his team to the professionals' quarters and bring [them] out into the field in a body, just for all the world as they were all flesh and blood. Many of us closed our eyes. We felt that Bolshevism had invaded our sanctuary.'

Widely regarded as the most astute and enterprising leader of his day, Fender's lack of recognition by the national selectors is commonly attributed to his presumed Jewishness and manifest lack of breeding (he was a wine trader without a university degree, for heaven's sake). It seems far more plausible that his flagrant disregard for the natural order ruffled too many feathers. Not until 1953 did Len Hutton become England's first professional captain.

Highest fourth-innings total to win
First-class: 507 for 7 (Cambridge University v MCC and Ground, Lord's, 1896)
Test: 406 for 4 (India v West Indies, Port of Spain, 1976)

Most runs in match (aggregate)
First-class: 2,376 (Maharashtra v Bombay, 1948–9)
Test: 1,981 (South Africa v England, 1939)

Most runs in a day (aggregate)
First-class: 721 (Australians v Essex, 1948)
Test: 588 (England v India, 1936)

Inside the Game

Long before the advent of international tours, the annual Gentlemen v Players contretemps at Lord's was the highlight of the English season. Not until 1962 was the fixture scrapped and the distinction abolished. At long last, or so we were assured, cricket's Feudal Age was over. The Industrial Revolution followed on cue.

Highway '81 Revisited: Robert ('Bob') George Dylan Willis

Lowest total (all 10 wickets down)
First-class: 12 (Northamptonshire v Gloucestershire, 1907)
Test: 26 (New Zealand v England, 1955)
Women
Test: 35 (England v Australia, 1958)

Fewest runs in a complete day
First-class & Test: 95 (Pakistan v Australia, 1957)

Fewest runs in a match (two completed innings)
First-class: 34 (Border v Natal, 1959–60)
Test: 81 (South Africa v Australia, 1932)

Most wickets in a day
First-class: 16 first-class games completed in one day since 1900
Test: 27 (England v Australia, 1888)

Cricket

THE GREAT MATCH

DAY TWO
Headingley, 17 July 1981

Score at start of play: Australia 203 for 3

'Botham 6-95 but Australians Grind On'
(Daily Telegraph)

Kim Hughes is not a captain who commands respect. Nor has earning it been easy. 'Whatever you think of him', Dennis Lillee once said, 'a couple of things are obvious: he is neither a transparent personality, nor a shrinking violet. Overconfidence has been one of his problems.' All the more reason, then, for Lillee and his fellow Australians to swallow their reservations and toast their leader. After all, but for his diligent, uncharacteristically restrained knock of 89, England might have had reason to believe they were back in a match that appears to have slithered from their grasp.

'Absorbing' is the word invariably resorted to by reporters confronted by days like this. But let's be frank: a guided tour of a morgue would have been less deathly. With almost two hours lost to the elements, the extra hour came into operation, prolonging the agony past seven o'clock.

Amid it all, Botham produced an inspired spell of five for thirty-five after tea, a runaway rhino full of snorting hostility. It was the first time he had taken that many wickets in an innings since Bombay 1980, which by coincidence – or otherwise –

115

happened to be his last game in the ranks. Leave it to me, he had told Brearley, I'll get you five. Unfortunately, our born-again derring-doer has probably left it a day and a half late.

When play resumed, Dilley took the new ball after three overs but his radar was awry. So much so that when Bright, the nightwatchman, was finally bowled by a straight one – having previously had his private parts jangled by a brute of a delivery – the element of surprise must have been quite considerable. Willis and Old were similarly undemanding; that their combined 438 deliveries in the innings yielded just 163 runs was deceptive as well as flattering.

Even Brearley's seemingly inexhaustible patience must have been in need of refuelling. On a pitch made for seam bowlers of such proven quality, the sight of batsmen blithely allowing ball after ball to sail harmlessly by doubtless caused Alderman and Lillee to snigger long and hard as they contemplated the havoc they would undoubtedly wreak when their turn came.

Joined by the lean, left-handed Yallop, Hughes occasionally availed us of some of his trademark flourishes, including some sumptuous cover drives off front foot and back, but pragmatism was the keynote. The 112-run stand he and Yallop compiled for the fifth wicket was painstaking, and all the more painful for being so alien to the nature of both partners.

Such wariness, mind, was eminently understandable. One ball from Willis to Hughes reared shoulder-high from only fractionally short of a length; then, half an hour after tea, Botham charged in to bruise his manhood. The spiritual damage was evident from Botham's next ball, when Hughes, after four and a half hours of dedication and self-denial, lobbed a gentle half-volley back to the exultant bowler. It was just the stroke of fortune Botham needed, spurring him on to heights he must have feared he might never attain again. You could already see the headlines: Superman Saved By Crushed Balls.

The truth was somewhat more prosaic, albeit a tribute to Brearley's psychological expertise. In his efforts to obtain more swing, Botham had been experimenting with a new technique in which he would shift sideways just before reaching his delivery stride, angling the ball in. 'Brears thought it had taken some of the pace and zip out of my bowling; he wanted me to bring the experiment to a close and just put my back into bowling fast. He even wound me up by calling me the "Sidestep Queen". I got the message ... with pretty decent results.'

Pretty decent, but nowhere near, one suspects, decent enough. On a two-paced pitch of uneven bounce, a total of 400 would appear to be about as reliable an insurance against defeat as an action replay of the Ten Plagues. Or, as Hughes himself put it, 'as good as a thousand'.

FOR THE NATIONAL HEALTH

It would be silly to pretend that the world fell in love at first sight. 'The Englishman carries his bat with him as naturally as his gun-case and his india-rubber bath', observed *Blackwood's Magazine* in 1892. In *Cricket Its Theory and Practice* (1868), however, Charles Box had poked fun at the export drive, outlining why the game was in no danger whatsoever of travelling well:

'The game is essentially English, and though our countrymen carry it abroad wherever they go, it is difficult to inoculate or knock it into the foreigner. The Italians are too fat for cricket, the French too thin, the Dutch too dumpy, the Belgians too bilious, the Flemish too flatulent, the East Indians too peppery, the Laplanders too bow-legged, the Swiss too sentimental, the Greeks too lazy, the Egyptians too long in the neck, and the Germans too short in the wind.'

Even in territories where the English could impose their culture, the inoculation process was far from smooth. The contrast to the rapid growth of the country's other prime sporting export, football, was marked indeed. Within fifty years of the inception of the Football Association (1863), sixteen countries outside England were operating their own national leagues; not until the end of the nineteenth century, 150 years after the laws had been drawn up, did there emerge any counterparts to the county championship.

In 1806, it was reported that a match in Sydney between British army regiments had drawn a crowd of 2,000; in 1824, their compatriots were reported to have played in Rangoon; by the 1830s, the game

---

Longest Test
10 days South Africa v England, Durban, 1939

Earliest finish
1.55 on second day, i.e. before lunch: England v Australia, 1888

Shortest Test (weather-affected)
49 mins – Sri Lanka 24 for 0 (12 overs) v India, 1993

Shortest Test (dangerous pitch)
57 mins – England 17 for 3 (10.1 overs) v West Indies, 1998

NB. Ten Tests have been cancelled or abandoned without a ball being bowled, five owing to political conditions/civil disturbances, five due to rain.

was flourishing in North America, home of the first international fixture, USA v Canada (1844), and the inaugural tour (by an English party in 1859); in 1855, the Bloemfontein club was founded in Orange Free State, South Africa, at a time when the population was estimated at little more than 100. The immediate priority of every new township in Australia, or so it appeared, was a racecourse and a cricket ground. In each case, the Anglo-Saxon influence was all-pervasive.

Much the most far-reaching development was the formation of the Oriental CC in 1848 by a small community of Parsees in Bombay. Up to then, all the impetus and enthusiasm had stemmed from the throne of Empire; granted, the Calcutta club had been founded at Eden Gardens in the late eighteenth century, yet its members remained exclusively English. Now, for the first time, the locals were sufficiently smitten to band together in their own right. An account of the period by Shapoorjee Sorabjee, published in 1897, mentions 'quaint bats unskilfully hewn out of old logs or cut out of planks that once served as lids or bottoms of dealwood boxes'. Come 1870, another Parsee club, Mars CC, even had the audacity to challenge Captain Cotton's 95th Regiment. They may have been trounced for their temerity, but the seeds had been sown in fertile soil.

The game's growth had taken another sizeable leap forward in 1861, with the first English tour of the Antipodes, even if some of the leading county professionals refused to take part because of the low pay. The rewards were duly increased for the next such venture two winters later, resulting in even more lopsided results. More significantly, two of the all-conquering 1861–2 tourists stayed in

INDIVIDUAL

Most Test appearances:
156 Allan Border
(Australia, 1978–94)

BATTING

Highest individual score
First-class: 501 not out
Brian Lara (Warwickshire v Durham, 1994)
Test: 375 Brian Lara
(West Indies v England, 1994)
Women: 224 not out
Mabel Bryant (Visitors v Residents, 1901)
Test: 204 Kirsty Flavell
(New Zealand v England, 1996)

Australia to coach, one of whom, Charles Lawrence, nurtured the game among the Aboriginals and in 1868 brought his pupils to England, where displays of spear- and boomerang-throwing proved the main attraction.

The 1873–4 English tour of Australia typified the early difficulties. Led by W.G. Grace, the twelve-man expedition left Southampton by ship on 23 October, arrived nearly eight weeks later, played fifteen three-day games against the odds (the opposition were always allowed to field more players, often as many as twenty-two) and eventually returned on 17 May, after the start of the domestic season. With a number of notable players unimpressed by a fee of £170 for what was effectively seven months' duty, WG's side comprised seven professionals and five amateurs (the latter, naturally, were billeted in first-class hotels).

'It was most unfortunate for the team', noted one member of the touring party, 'that they should have fallen into the hands of 12 speculators, all of whom were in business of some sort or another, and, I am sorry to say, knew really nothing of cricket ... they actually wanted us to commence at two o'clock on the third day. The trip ... was not a great one. We were met in a bad spirit, as if contending cricketers were great enemies.'

Although fixtures such as Smokers v Non-Smokers still proliferated, Australia's burgeoning sense of nationalism led to the creation of a representative team (albeit at first drawn exclusively from Melbourne and Sydney), which helped in no small measure to unify the rival states. In due course came what is regarded as the inaugural 'Test'

Highest average
Career
First-class: 95.14 Don Bradman (New South Wales, South Australia & Australia, 1927–48)
Test: 99.94 Don Bradman

Season
First-class: (min. 1,000 runs) 177.87 Vijay Hazare (Baroda, 1943–4)

Series
Test: (min. 500 runs) 201.50 Don Bradman (v South Africa, 1931–2)

match. The term was coined by journalists to commemorate a game staged at the Melbourne Cricket Ground from 15 March to 19 March 1877 (18 March was the designated 'rest' day): it was, after all, the first time an Australian team had been deemed worthy enough to meet their English counterparts on an even footing, i.e. eleven-a- side.

(Historical footnote: since the term was coined by journalists, who kept the early records, the sixtieth 'Test', between England and Australia at Nottingham in 1899, was the first of any official stature. Never before had an England XI been nominated by an official team of selectors.)

Whatever the status of the contest, Australia were the winners (eerily enough, the margin of forty-five runs would be repeated when the protagonists celebrated a century of conflict on the same ground in 1977). Another game was hastily arranged, and captain James Lillywhite's charges reasserted their assumed superiority. Which prompted accusations that they had purposely lost the original contest, according to one of their number, Alfred Shaw, 'in order to obtain another game and gate'. Not for another thirty-one years would England's football team play their first fixture outside Britain.

South Africa were admitted to the club in the winter of 1888–9; as with the Australians, their home Tests were played to a finish, though since the matting pitches there were so helpful to bowlers these seldom exceeded three days. There were to be no further additions for forty years; even when the field expanded either side of the Second World War, it did so grudgingly: Zimbabwe became No. 9 in 1991.

To date, astonishing as it may seem, there has never

Most runs
Career
First-class: 61,237 Jack Hobbs (Surrey & England, 1905–34)
Test: 11,174 Allan Border (Australia)

Women
Test: 1,594 Rachel Heyhoe-Flint (England, 1960–79)

Season
First-class: 3,814 Denis Compton (Middlesex & England, 1947)

Series
Test: 974 Don Bradman (v England, 1930)

Inside the Game

been any real attempt to determine a world champion. The logistics, of course, would be horrendous, albeit not insuperable (but more of that anon). Aside from the limited-overs World Cup, the closest approximation was the Triangular Tournament between England, Australia and South Africa in the bliss-free summer of 1912. Three of the nine Tests were washed out.

It was an indication of Australian passions that when the first official tour party arrived in England in 1878 all but one member was native-born. Between then and 1890, they crossed hemispheres every other summer. Not that they were always welcomed with unreserved warmth. 'We had to make some protest against too frequent visits', reasoned Lord Harris, the autocrat hailed by some to be the game's most significant administrator and missionary, who saw to it that the visitors played comparatively few games in 1880 when they turned up at two weeks' notice. That August, in a gesture of conciliation, Harris consented to the first 'Test' on English soil; held at the Kennington Oval, south London. England won with comparative ease inside the allotted three days – a resounding victory for captain Harris!

Two years later, Australia triumphed at the Oval, paving the way for the inception of the Ashes. The motivation was obvious: Australians liked nothing more than cocking a snook at the stiff-upper-lipped 'Hinglish', an entirely natural source of inspiration that would subsequently embolden the rest of the Dominions; for the Poms to put the Cobbers and their baggy green caps to flight was to keep the peasants in their place. Few holds were barred. In the first Test of the 1897–8 series – reports of which were cabled to Queen Victoria – Australia's Charles McLeod was bowled by a no ball; unfortunately,

Most centuries
Career
First-class: 197 Jack Hobbs
Test: 34 Sunil Gavaskar (India, 1970–87)

Season
First-class: 18 Denis Compton (1947)

Series
Test: 5 Clyde Walcott (West Indies v Australia, 1955)

Fastest centuries (balls received; against legitimate bowling)
First-class: 34 David Hookes (South Australia v Victoria, 1982)
Test: 56 Viv Richards (West Indies v England, 1986)

being deaf, he didn't hear the umpire's call, assumed he was out and strode off. Not one English fielder saw fit to put him straight.

And then came 'The Don'. If the expansion of Test cricket in the late 1920s and early 1930s reflected the wider surge in nationalism (West Indies, New Zealand and India all came aboard, doubling the field), no sportsman did more to promote a sense of national identity and pride than Donald George Bradman. Coinciding as they did with Australia's Depression years of the early 1930s, the staggering feats of batsmanship from this slightly-built farmer's son from the New South Wales backwoods supplied both an escape route and a focus for aspiration, accompanied as they invariably were by a sound thrashing for the Poms. Like WG, 'The Don's' very presence could double the crowd, a goodly proportion of whom would file out once he was dismissed. The title of one popular contemporary song summed it up perfectly: 'Our Don Bradman'.

He had his detractors, of course. To the English he was too relentless, too ruthless, not to mention too damn good. The legendary England opener, Jack Hobbs, aka 'The Master', scorer of more runs than anyone in first-class cricket will ever score, accused him of spoiling the game. 'He got too many runs. The pot calling the kettle black? No, I was human ... He was mechanical ... I do not think we want to see another one quite like him.' As a captain Bradman was no less remorseless and unyielding, attributing his philosophy to the tactics he observed in his first Test: 'England, though leading by nearly 400, went in again [instead of enforcing the follow-on] and left us over 700 to attempt in our last innings with two men out of

Most runs off over
First-class: 36 (off six balls; six sixes) Garfield Sobers (Nottinghamshire v Glamorgan, 1968); Ravi Shastri (Bombay v Baroda, 1985)
Test: 25 (off eight balls) Bert Sutcliffe and Bob Blair (New Zealand v South Africa, 1953)

Longest before scoring first run
First-class & Test: 1hr 37 minutes Godfrey Evans (England v Australia, 1947)

Longest scoreless spell
First-class: 2hrs 11 mins Shoaib Mohammad (Karachi Blues v Lahore City Whites, 1983)
Test: 1hr 34 mins Martin Snedden (New Zealand v Australia, 1989)

action.' The blackguard in question was the hard-drinking cavalier from Kent, Percy Chapman, allegedly an officer and a Gentleman.

Then came Bodyline. Originally known as 'leg-theory', this was the name given to a manoeuvre wherein the bowler fired the ball in short, aiming to bounce it at the batsman's body, then wait for him to fend it off towards an array of hovering fielders on the leg side. In 1925, *The Cricketer* magazine, edited by 'Plum' Warner, attacked it for being 'a confession of impotence on the part of the bowler, and that should serve to cut it out of the game of any and every bowler claiming to be first class'.

The storm broke during the MCC tour of Australia in the winter of 1932–3, when Douglas Jardine, the England captain, following the lead of Arthur Carr, the Nottinghamshire skipper, employed it to curb the threat of Bradman and hence retrieve the Ashes. In achieving those ends – the Don averaged a relatively piffling 56, well shy of his previous mark of 139.14 – Jardine and his chosen agent of destruction, the deadly and obedient Nottinghamshire paceman Harold Larwood, were responsible for the least savoury, most divisive episode in the game's history. Addressing a lunch, J.H. Thomas, Secretary of State for the Dominions, conveyed his frustrations: 'No politics ever introduced in the British Empire ever caused me so much trouble as this damn Bodyline bowling.'

Dubbed 'the Iron Duke', Jardine detested Australians and wore a garish Harlequin cap as a means of provocation. Like many, he perceived the Australians as being far too keen to win. Like many, he saw this as a threat to the amateur ideal. He was also spurred by the humiliations of 1930, when

---

Slowest century
First-class & Test: 9hrs 17 mins Mudassar Nazar (Pakistan v England, 1977)

Longest innings
First-class & Test: 337 in 16hrs 10mins Hanif Mohammad (Pakistan v West Indies, 1958)

Partnerships for each wicket

1st
First-class: 561 Waheed Mirza and Mansoor Akhtar (Karachi Whites v Quetta, 1977)
Test: 413 Vinoo Mankad and Pankaj Roy (India v New Zealand, 1956)

2nd
First-class & Test: 576 Sanath Jayasurya and Roshan Mahanama (Sri Lanka v India, 1997)

Cricket

Villainous hero: Harold Larwood, obedient arch-exponent of Bodyline

Bradman had more or less beaten England on his own. This time it was personal. 'Few will be found to admit', averred Jardine somewhat pointedly, 'that the hero-worship to which, for example, Bradman was subject, is desirable for the game's good.'

Not every member of the England team agreed with Bodyline. 'Gubby' Allen, a key fast bowler, refused to follow orders (mind you, his amateur status made it easier for him to uphold his principles). In Larwood and his Nottinghamshire colleague Bill Voce, however, Jardine had a pair of dutiful pros.

In Adelaide, Bill Woodfull, Australia's intensely religious captain, was struck a sickening blow over

3rd
First-class & Test: 467 Andrew Jones and Martin Crowe (New Zealand v Sri Lanka, 1990)

4th
First-class: 577 Vijay Hazare and Gul Mahomed (Baroda v Holkar, 1947)
Test: 411 Peter May and Colin Cowdrey (England v West Indies, 1957)

5th
First-class: 464 (unbroken) Mark and Steve Waugh (New South Wales v Western Australia, 1990–1)
Test: 405 Sid Barnes and Don Bradman (Australia v England, 1946)

the heart. He made his objections quite clear to the tour manager, who just happened to be none other than dear old Plum. 'I don't want to see you Mr Warner', the normally placid Woodfull fumed as he lay on the treatment table. 'There are two teams out there; one is trying to play cricket and the other is not.'

Jardine was depicted as Satan's nastier brother, his players abused in the street and vilified in the music hall. The word 'Bodyline' passed into popular usage, embodying the very essence of all that was underhand (and quite plainly 'not cricket'). Amid the heated diplomatic exchanges that ensued, the Australian Cricket Board dispatched an angry cable to Lord's. 'Unless stopped at once', it warned, '[this tactic] is likely to upset the friendly relationship existing between Australia and England.' The Earl of Dartmouth, one of the MCC's leading mandarins, was moved to verse:

6th
First-class: 487 (unbroken) George Headley and Clarence Passailaigue (Jamaica v Lord Tennyson's XI, 1931–2)
Test: 346 Jack Fingleton and Don Bradman (Australia v England, 1937)

7th
First-class: 460 Bhupinder Singh Jr and P Dharmani (Punjab v Delhi, 1994–5)
Test: 347 Denis Atkinson and Clairmonte Depeiza (West Indies v Australia, 1955)

We have fought
We have won
And we have lost
But we have never squealed before

Although the Earl's more enlightened colleagues saw to it that Bodyline was quickly outlawed – a restriction of two fielders behind the wicket on the leg side was imposed – Jardine retained the England captaincy until his retirement in 1934. Larwood, the lowly miner, was made the scapegoat. Never again did he wear his country's colours. He became an outcast, a scar removed.

Not unexpectedly, a certain amount of dramatic licence was in evidence in the Australian TV series, *Bodyline*. For one thing, 'Bradman' was portrayed as tall, dark and handsome: nought out of three. Jane Larwood certainly wasn't convinced about the verisimilitude: 'I'm sure my father wasn't a pisspot and a yobbo.'

Forgiving foe: Jack Fingleton (right) walks out to bat with Stan McCabe

A year or so later, Bradman was restored to immortality and Australia retrieved the Ashes; they have held the upper hand ever since. During their triumphant march through England in 1948, Larwood had a drink in Blackpool with one of his Bodyline foes, Jack Fingleton, now cricket correspondent of London's *Sunday Times*, a man he had come perilously close to maiming. The pair had been corresponding for years. 'Larwood was living in complete obscurity', noted Fingleton in his diary. 'Disillusioned, felt unwanted ... could not be induced to talk of cricket.' Two years later, Larwood sent him an imploring telegram:

Leaving London Tomorrow Stop Can You Arrange Accommodation For Self Wife Five Daughters Eldest Daughter's Fiance Stop Also Jobs

Fingleton had a few words in the right ears and all was arranged. Larwood spent the rest of his days Down Under, welcome and forgiven, an enduring symbol of the healing powers of a common affliction.

8th
First-class: 433 Victor Trumper and A. Sims (A. Sims' Australian XI v Canterbury, 1913–14)
Test: 313 Wasim Akram and Saqlain Mushtaq (Pakistan v Zimbabwe, 1997)

9th
First-class: 283 John Chapman and Arnold Warren (Derbyshire v Warwickshire, 1910)
Test: 199 Mark Boucher and Pat Symcox (South Africa v Pakistan, 1998)

10th
First-class: 307 Alan Kippax and Hal Hooker (New South Wales v Victoria, 1928)
Test: 151 Brian Hastings and Richard Collinge (New Zealand v Pakistan, 1973)

THE GREAT MATCH

DAY THREE
Headingley, 18 July 1981

Score at start of play: Australia 401 for nine declared; England 7 for 0

'Contentious Rule gives England Breathing Space' (Daily Telegraph)

The beast stirs. For the first time in twenty Test innings, Botham made a half-century, and with the panache of old. Unfortunately for England, Alderman and Lillee, abetted by the raw pace of Lawson, proved every bit as obstructive as expected.

Behind Botham, who thrashed his round, robust fifty off just seventy-five balls, England's next highest scorer was David Gower, who suffered a horrid blow to the ribs from Lawson and wound up with a fraught twenty-four; nobody else passed fifteen on a pitch lambasted by Peter Philpott, Australia's manager, as 'a disgrace'. With a lead of 227, Hughes enforced the follow-on and asked England to face the music again. When Graham Gooch completed the unenviable feat of being out twice in the same day without bothering the scorers, the requiem was in full swing.

Amid all the submissiveness, Botham provided the only respite. Credited by one member of the Australian party, Rodney Hogg, with having 'a degree in people', Brearley was a major – albeit silent – source of encouragement. 'He looked up to the players' balcony and saw me. I grinned broadly, and gestured that he should have tried to hit it even harder, thereby conveying, I hoped, my pleasure at his uninhibited approach and an unqualified approval of his continuing in an extravagant vein.'

It couldn't last, and didn't. Celebrating his thirty-second birthday, Lillee produced a spitting delivery that brushed Botham's gloves en route to those of Marsh, who pouched the catch and hurled it in the general direction of kingdom come. He, too, had cause for rejoicing: it was his 264th victim for Australia, outstripping Alan Knott's Test wicketkeeping record.

The end of the day was thoroughly unpleasant. Bad light forced the combatants off the field shortly after Gooch's second dismissal, and although they returned for four overs, it was still deemed too gloomy by the umpires come six o'clock. Since regulations state that, for the extra hour to be taken, conditions must be fit at the scheduled close of play, Messrs Meyer and Evans were fully entitled to call a halt; the disgruntled crowd, however, were more than a little miffed when, three minutes later, the sun burst out. And stayed out. Cushions were thrown; some vowed never to return.

Cricket's fine print, pernickety at the best of times, has seldom been a match for the wilful vagaries of a British summer. Still, given the home team's plight, you might have imagined the assembled throng would have been grateful for being spared any further humiliation. We Poms truly are the best of sports.

APOCALYPSE DELAYED

A FEW days prior to the 1896 Ashes Test at the Oval, five members of the England team threatened to strike over pay. Three relented; William Gunn and George Lohmann, the most prodigious Test bowler of all time, went the whole hog. Neither was called to arms again.

In 1912, a power struggle in Australia between the professionals and the Board of Control led to six leading players pulling out of the impending Triangular Tournament in England, the game's first attempt to stage a world championship. During one famously turbulent selection meeting, Peter McAlister and Clem Hill, the Australian captain, came to blows.

Incidents of this nature are worth mentioning because of their scarcity value. All right, so Bobby Peel, the first great Yorkshire left-arm spinner, was fabled for his drinking prowess (legend has it that he was sacked for urinating on the pitch), but, by and large, as befitted their supposedly inferior status, the Players were orderly, obedient coves. The Cricketers' Association, the first players' union (discounting the largely mythical 'fast bowlers' union'), did not emerge until 1967, four years after the pros had gained equal rights. Militants in the making? Pah. Or so their bosses thought. Kerry Packer made them think again.

It seems only apt that the post-amateur era should have begun in the same season that brought the world its first major limited-overs tournament. In that one English summer, or so it appeared, the past was left behind, the future embraced.

BOWLING

Highest Test career strike rate (balls per wicket; min. 50 wickets)
34.11 George Lohmann (England, 1886–96)

Best analysis
Innings
First-class: 10 for 10 Hedley Verity (Yorkshire v Nottinghamshire, 1932)
Test: 10 for 53 Jim Laker (England v Australia, 1956)

Most wickets
Match
First-class & Test: 19 Jim Laker (England v Australia, 1956)

Career
First-class: 4,187 Wilfred Rhodes (Yorkshire & England, 1898–1930)
Test: 434 Kapil Dev (India; 1978-93)

Cricket

There can be little doubt that the 1963 season was the most significant in the game's history thus far. On 19 April, a week after Martin Luther King had been arrested for leading a civil rights march in Alabama, at the very height of the Profumo Crisis, came the publication of the 100th edition of *Wisden Cricketers' Almanack* ('LIMP COVERS AT TWENTY-TWO SHILLINGS AND SIXPENCE NET, CLOTH BOARDS BINDING AT TWENTY-FIVE SHILLINGS NET'). 'I don't think I am giving away any secrets', wrote its editor Norman Preston, 'when I say that even the publisher was surprised by the demand ... It ran into three impressions before everyone was satisfied.'

All this was interpreted as proof of cricket's anointed and inviolate place in the English psyche, at a time when the evidence had rarely been less compelling. With the exception of one magical Test series between West Indies and Australia, the game had become tepid and turgid. The disappearance of the amateur captain was touted as a root cause. Players seemed oblivious to the purpose or even existence of spectators.

Find a copy of the 1997 *Wisden* (1,442 pages, price £26, less if soft cover), turn to page 241 and check out Test cricket's Hall of Shamelessness, namely the list headed 'Fewest Runs In A Full Day's Play' (i.e. five or more hours). Five of the top six, ranging from 95 right up to the giddy heights of 117, occurred between 1956 and 1959. At Brisbane in 1958, Trevor 'Barnacle' Bailey took more than seven and a half hours to score sixty-eight. 'It requires an earthquake', warranted one long-time colleague, 'to make him change his game in midstream.' C.L.R. James described it as 'the welfare state of mind'.

Season
First-class: 304 Alfred 'Tich' Freeman (Kent, 1928)

Series
Test: 49 Sydney Barnes (England v South Africa, 1913–14)

Most productive spell
First-class: 7 wickets in 11 balls Pat Pocock (Surrey v Sussex, 1972)
Test: 4 wickets in 5 balls Maurice Allom (England v New Zealand, 1930); Chris Old (England v Pakistan, 1978); Wasim Akram (Pakistan v West Indies, 1990)

Lowest average (runs per wicket)
Career
First-class: (min. 1,000 wickets) 12.12 Alfred Shaw (Nottinghamshire, Sussex & England, 1864–97)
Test: (min. 100 wickets) 10.75 George Lohmann

Inside the Game

In February 1963, the Ashes series had ended all-square after the fifth Test in Sydney, neither side having strained themselves unduly to force victory. Here was the welfare state of mind at its zenith: make sure you can't lose and then – and only then – contemplate taking a risk. Since England had to win the match to regain the urn, this was especially unforgiveable. 'The deciding match of the series', lamented *Wisden*, 'far from being the exciting contest expected, turned out to be a dull, lifeless game which did immense harm to cricket ... On most of the days there was a good deal of barracking and the game ended with booing and slow-handclapping.'

As luck would have it, the northern hemisphere season of 1963 turned out to be the most vibrant for yonks. John Wisden & Co, 'the proprietors', commemorated the centenary of their yellow 'Bible' with the Wisden Trophy, to be competed for in Test series between England and West Indies. On 26 August, Frank Worrell held the sparkling new pot aloft at the Oval, worthy reward for a summer dominated by the searing pace of Wes Hall and Charlie Griffith, the artful spin of Lance Gibbs, the exuberant batting of Rohan Kanhai and the unique, unadulterated genius of Garfield Sobers. A summer, too, in which Britain's Caribbean immigrants at last found a voice (even if they did employ it to cheer on the opposition).

The most important date was still 7 September, the day Sussex won the inaugural Knockout Competition final at Lord's. A single-day, single-innings, 65-overs-per-side affair (with bowlers confined to 15 apiece), it was lapped up by a full house of 23,000; it was reportedly the first cricket match ever to sell out in advance. Five days later,

Season
First-class: (min. 50 wickets) 6.81 Ron Oxenham (Australians in South Africa, 1935–6)

Series
Test: (min. 15 wickets) 5.80 George Lohmann (England v South Africa, 1895–6)

Most economical (Test career; min. 2,000 balls) 21.96 runs per 100 balls William Attewell (England, 1884–92)

Most runs conceded
Innings
First-class: 362 Arthur Mailey (New South Wales v Victoria, 1926)
Test: 298 Leslie 'Chuck' Fleetwood-Smith (Australia v England, 1938)

Sussex upset the West Indians in a fifty-five overs-a-side, one-day 'Challenge match'. How nigh-on 15,000 people were shoehorned into Hove remains a source of wonder to this day.

Two attempts were made that summer to resurrect the first-class game's flagging appeal in the shires. One was the Better Cricket Competition, launched by the *Daily Express* to celebrate the *Wisden* centenary. Proposals from readers ranged from bonus points to encourage faster scoring to the introduction of Sunday cricket after church, complete with two divisions, promotion and relegation. Then there was the Knockout Competition, organised by the counties purely as an experiment. The concept could hardly be faulted: guarantee the public a complete match – and a result – in one day (weather permitting). And no draws. In striving to secure its future, cricket had drawn inspiration from its origins.

The next year saw changes rung: the sixty-five overs were pared back to sixty, five minor counties were invited to participate and Gillette, the razor people, stepped in as backers. The event was renamed the Gillette Cup, ushering in the age of commercial sponsorship. The John Player Sunday League followed in 1969, the Benson & Hedges Cup in 1972. From Weston super Mare to West Hartlepool, new converts flocked along, folk who'd never attended a championship match in their lives. Younger, less reserved, less patient. Families attended after church.

Elsewhere, the gratitude was less obvious. To the various national boards, this bastardised, bowdlerised version of their precious plaything was a necessary evil at best. Not until 1971 – and

Match
First-class: 428 Cottari Nayudu (Holkar v Bombay, 1945)
Test: 374 Oscar 'Tommy' Scott (West Indies v England, 1930)

Most balls bowled
Innings
First-class & Test: 588 Sonny Ramadhin (West Indies v England, 1957)

Match
First-class: 917 Cottari Nayudu (Holkar v Bombay, 1945)
Test: 774 Sonny Ramadhin (West Indies v England, 1957)

Inside the Game

Ringmaster: Kerry Packer

ALL-ROUNDERS

Career
First-class: 54,896 runs and 2,876 wickets W.G. Grace (Gloucestershire & England, 1865–1908)
Test: 5,248 runs and 434 wickets Kapil Dev

Season
First-class: 2,385 runs and 208 wickets George Hirst (Yorkshire, 1906)

then only because a Test match in Melbourne had been abandoned – was the first one-day international staged. It was if the authorities believed the new drug, with its side-effects of negative bowling and crude batting, would be hazardous to health. They certainly feared it would be hazardous to tradition.

Cue the inaugural World Cup in 1975, sponsored by Prudential Assurance and held in England. Helpfully, the fates took a hand. The sun shone when it mattered, the West Indies edged past Pakistan at Edgbaston thanks to an improbable last-wicket stand of sixty-four and little Alvin Kallicharran smashed dastardly Dennis Lillee all over the Oval. Not even the home team's loss to Australia in the semi-finals could dampen local enthusiasm. Best of all, Lord's was bathed in sun for the final and Clive Lloyd did the occasion proud with a majestic century, leading the West Indies to victory in one of the most riveting contests ever to grace grass. The winners boogied into the smallest hours. Dollar signs danced before Kerry Packer's eyes.

Kerry Francis Bullmore Packer is averse to doing things by halves. The Packers always have been. Granddad was broke when he found ten shillings at a racetrack in Tasmania, bet the lot and won six pounds, enough to pay his passage to the more verdant pastures of Sydney. Before reinventing himself as one of Australia's most indomitable press barons, Sir Frank, Kerry's arrogant, determined, tartar of a father, had been heavyweight champion of New South Wales. Many was the time an errant Kerry would be summoned to the drawing-room, gloves at the ready.

A hulking 6ft 1, 18-stone milkshake-lover, Kerry had assumed control of the Packer portfolio in 1974. He smoked up to four packs of cigarettes a day, having given up the drinking and heavy gambling on account of being, as he himself put it, 'incapable of moderation'. Cricket was simply a convenient vehicle for his ambitions. By 1976, he had transformed the family business, selling off newspapers and relaunching into magazines and TV. When he approached the Australian Cricket Board with a handsome offer for exclusive rights to broadcast Test matches on his own Channel 9 network, he wasn't simply backing a hunch. The world's best team were on his doorstep.

The ACB turned its nose up. The Australian Broadcasting Corporation had been a loyal servant, the board explained, less than convincingly. Who knew what indecencies this vulgarian might perpetrate? Blunt as ever, Packer snapped back: 'There is a little bit of a whore in all of us, gentlemen.'

Packers, however, are not easily thwarted, hence Kerry's decision to bankroll a rival to the official product. World Series Cricket was the official brand name, Kerry Packer's Flying Circus its most popular *nom de guerre*. 'Genghis Khan wasn't very loveable but he was bloody efficient', was one of the ringmaster's pearls, prompting *Spitting Image*, a satirical British TV show, to portray him as the genocidally-inclined Mongol. Genghis Packer's soundest bite? No contest: 'Cricket is the easiest sport in the world to take over. Nobody bothered to pay the players what they were worth.'

Greg Chappell was the biggest catch. Without the captain and prime batsman, the other dozen

Series
Test: 545 runs and 29 wickets Aubrey Faulkner (South Africa v England, 1909–10);
475 runs and 34 wickets George Giffen (Australia v England, 1894–5);
722 runs and 20 wickets Garfield Sobers (West Indies v England, 1966)

Match
First-class: 271, 9 for 96 and 7 for 70 George Giffen (South Australia v Victoria, 1891–2);
Test: 114, 6 for 58 and 7 for 48 Ian Botham (England v India, 1980)

FIELDING

Most victims
(wicketkeeper; catches and stumpings)

Career
First-class: 1,649 Bob Taylor (Derbyshire & England, 1960–88)
Test: 355 Rodney Marsh (Australia, 1970–83)

Season
First-class: 128 Les Ames (Kent, 1929)

Series
Test: 28 Rodney Marsh (Australia v England, 1982–3)

Inside the Game

Part-time king: Greg Chappell

Match
First-class: 13 (2 stumped) Wayne James (Matabeleland v Mashonaland Central Districts, 1996)
Test: 11 (all caught) Robert 'Jack' Russell (England v South Africa, 1995)

Innings
First-class: 9 Tahir Rashid (Habib Bank v PACO, 1992; 1 stumped), Wayne James (Matabeleland v Mashonaland CD, 1996; 2 stumped);
Test: 7 (all caught) Bob Taylor (England v India, 1980); Wasim Bari (Pakistan v New Zealand, 1979)

Australian 'rebels' due to tour England in 1977 might have lost their nerve. Without Chappell, the pirate ship Packer might never have set sail. As it was, England regained the Ashes against opponents whose minds were seldom wholly on the job.

If there was ever to be a meaningful revolt, it was always going to start in the southern hemisphere. Like most non-English practitioners, Chappell was a part-timer. The five-month Ashes tour of 1972 had earned him the princely sum of A$2,000, *before* tax; in 1948, The Don and his men had received A$1,000, tax-free, enough to buy a house. 'After you'd taken tax out of $2,000', remarked Chappell's exasperated wife, Judy, 'you couldn't even put a *deposit* on a house.'

This imbalance had a fair deal to do with cricket's aversion to marketing (far too vulgar). With Test attendances on the wane amid a world of ever-shortening attention spans, it was even more symptomatic of a game, if not exactly on its knees, then decidedly unhip. It also symbolised the desire of the Gents to keep the Players firmly in their place.

Chappell's first inkling of a new dawn came during the Sydney Test of January 1976, when the mainstays of the Australian team had an informal chat at the Oxford Hotel with John Cornell, a TV star-turned-entrepreneur who had once played a character known as Strop. The gist of Cornell's thrust was clear: why should those old skinflints at the board reap all the fruits of your sweat?

Chappell listened intently but shrugged. There was no way the board was going to consent to their playing for a rival promoter. Besides, where would the money come from? He assumed he'd heard the last of it. The persuasive Cornell then joined forces with Austin Robertson, journalist and one-time Australian Rules Football luminary. Before long, they were wooing Packer.

Come February 1977, Packer was aboard. Not only that, Cornell and Robertson were discreetly boasting that they had the signatures of some forty players of world renown. When Cornell apprised him of this, Chappell was far more receptive. He would make up his mind by the Centenary Test. Little did the organisers of that lavish and emotional tribute to the past suspect the subplot.

Chappell wrote a note to himself, listing the pros: 'Shorter seasons – shorter tours – more money – less reliant on commercialism of self – more security ... minimal disruption to existing system – in fact complementing it ... alternative to a tyrannous regime.'

A few weeks later, cat bade farewell to bag. In late April, the South African *Sunday Times* published a leak: Mike Procter, Graeme Pollock and Barry Richards, so long denied a loftier stage by apartheid, had signed up for a series of unofficial exhibition games that winter. Ever cautious, Chappell feigned innocence on 7 May when a brace of reporters tackled him during a downpour at Hove. 'Sounds interesting', he replied, poker-faced. 'I'd like to know more about it.'

The following afternoon, Tony Greig, South African-born captain of Sussex and England, described by no more grudging distributor of compliments than Ray Illingworth as 'one of the most imposing and influential captains in the

Most stumpings

Career
First-class: 418 Les Ames (Kent & England, 1926–51)
Test: 52 Bill Oldfield (Australia, 1920–37)

Season
First-class: 64 Les Ames (1932)

Series
Test: 9 Percy Sherwell (South Africa v Australia, 1910–11)

Match
First-class: 9 Fred Huish (Kent v Surrey, 1911)
Test: 5 Kiran More (India v West Indies, 1988)

Innings
First-class: 6 Hugo Yarnold (Worcestershire v Scotland, 1951)
Test: 5 Kiran More (India v West Indies, 1988)

history of English cricket', issued a press statement that introduced Kerry Packer to the British public. To say that this sent the moggy hurtling into the pigeons would be an understatement. That winter, along with a number of English cricket's other leading lights, Greig would be part of 'a massive project involving most of the world's top players'. Within the week he was a former England captain. For a while, even his father refused to have anything to do with him.

Reactions veered between the snide, the hysterical and the blatantly racist. Tim Rice wondered 'if our handsome ex-captain is prepared to hawk his talents in any marketplace, would he like a role in Jesus Christ Superstar?' *The Times* unleashed its cricket correspondent's trenchant verdict on the front page. 'What has to be remembered of course is that he [Greig] is an Englishman, not by birth or upbringing, but only by adoption', thundered John Woodcock, by nature a sweet, reasonable human being. 'It is not the same as being an Englishman through and through.'

Greig was certainly in exalted company. When the identities of the first thirty-five 'rebels' were announced the next day, with precious few exceptions, everyone who was anyone was there: from the West Indies came Clive Lloyd, Andy Roberts, Michael Holding and Vivian Richards; from Pakistan, Mushtaq Mohammed, Imran Khan and Majid Khan. For Australians in possession of an open mind, the prospect of seeing Lillee launch his warheads at Pollock and Richards was enough to water the most dehydrated mouth.

The lure for Greig was plain. Basic tour fees were £3,000 (for roughly four months' work); home

---

Fielding Catches

Career
First-class: 1,018 Frank Woolley (Kent & England, 1906–38)
Test: 156 Allan Border

Season
First-class: 78 Walter Hammond (Gloucestershire & England, 1928)

Series
Test: 15 Jack Gregory (Australia v England, 1920–1)

Tests paid a niggardly £200 – rather small beer considering receipts from the forthcoming Jubilee Test at Lord's would raise a record £220,000. For a single winter's labours, Packer was offering up to five or six times as much. For all the cries of treachery, consciences were largely untroubled. 'It makes me laugh when I hear the anti-Packer lobby telling me how to spend my winters', said Gordon Greenidge, the Hampshire and West Indies opener. 'When I was a teenager, the same sort of people didn't give a damn what I did between September and April.'

The authorities were all but unanimous in their high-handed affront. Since the ICC's constituents controlled most of the grounds Packer could use, this was something of an obstacle. 'Regret communication with your good self improper', ran the cable from Pakistan. Only the West Indies dissented. One official from their perennially cash-strapped board let it be known that a couple of million dollars for bringing the circus to their town would not go amiss.

In June, Packer marched out of a stormy meeting with the ICC at Lord's and declared war: 'Had I got those TV rights I was prepared to withdraw from the scene. I now will take no steps to help anyone. Every man for himself and the devil take the hindmost.'

Then things got really nasty. On 26 July, to no one's great surprise, the ICC banned from Test cricket any player 'who after 1 October 1977 has played or made himself available to play in a match previously disapproved of by the Conference'. The Test and County Cricket Board ventured a step further on 10 August, stipulating that Packer

Match
First-class: 10 Walter Hammond (Gloucestershire v Surrey, 1928)
Test: 7 Greg Chappell (Australia v England, 1974); Yajurvindra Singh (India v England, 1977); Hashan Tillekeratne (Sri Lanka v England, 1993); Stephen Fleming (New Zealand v Australia, 1997)

Innings
First-class: 7 Tony Brown (Gloucestershire v Nottinghamshire, 1966); Mickey Stewart (Surrey v Northamptonshire, 1957)
Test: 5 Vic Richardson (Australia v South Africa, 1936); Yajurvindra Singh (India v England, 1977); Mohammad Azharuddin (India v Pakistan, 1989); Kris Srikkanth (India v Australia, 1992); Stephen Fleming (New Zealand v Australia, 1997)

players, a third of whom held county contracts, would be *persona non grata* in the shires. Quite which legal beagle advised them that this complied with the rules pertaining to restraint of trade remains uncertain, but the upshot was a sound thrashing in the High Court.

Greig, Procter and another Englishman, John Snow, duly sued the TCCB. On 28 November, after thirty-one days and a 221-page judgement that took five and a half hours to deliver, Justice Slade found for the plaintiffs, ordering the TCCB to pay costs of £200,000. Still, the defendants had just earned £150,000 for selling the Australian TV rights to the recent Ashes series – to Channel 9.

More significantly, Justice Slade defended the players' allegedly suspect morals: 'It is straining the concept of loyalty too far for authorities to expect [a player] to enter into a self-denying ordinance not to play for a private promoter ... merely because the matches could detract from the future profits made by the authorities, who are not willing or in a position to offer him employment in the future.'

'The problem from the outset', observed Ian Wooldridge in the *Daily Mail*, 'was that Establishment cricket was blinded by outrage. Its English administrators, most of whom cast their votes for private enterprise at the last election, panicked badly when actually confronted by it.' And shot itself in both feet.

Over the succeeding two winters, World Series Cricket operated in a vacuum, isolated by sanctioned Tests and media loathing. The early shows were mostly at football grounds, before

---

LIMITED-OVERS INTERNATIONALS

Due to the ever-increasing welter of such matches since their inception in 1971, records are often out of date before the ink has dried. Until comparatively recently, moreover, they did not conform to a standard duration (while the rest of the world had long since adopted a uniform fifty overs per side, England persisted with fifty-five until 1996). The advent of fielding circles, furthermore, has had a detrimental effect on bowling averages, which explains why Geoff Arnold, whose one-day career for England was over before the circles were introduced, still boasts the lowest average and economy rate. As of June 1998, the principal feats were as follows:

sparse throngs, but the advent of day/night limited-overs games lit the blue touchpaper. This was Packer's attempt to glean a share of the peak-time armchair audience and it worked a treat. He also devised fielding circles, to ease strokemaking and stop opposition captains littering their charges around the boundary: this was a batsman's game, too, only more so.

As the marketing began to kick in, as Joe and Joanne Public were seduced by the brash new technicolour world of white balls, black sightscreens, dayglo flannels and floodlights, so Packer gained access to the fortresses. The Sydney Cricket Ground took his money. Inch by painful inch, other concessions were made. Day by day, the market expanded.

The West Indies board betrayed its main agenda by offering to initiate dialogue between Packer and the ICC; sure enough, that WSC tour was soon in the pipeline. From England, too, came signs of shifting priorities. While many county wages doubled in the summer of 1978, a further ruse to ward off future defections saw Cornhill, a hitherto inconspicuous insurance firm, undertake to sponsor home Tests. Match fees soared to £1,000, a rise of 400 per cent. The bullet had been bitten.

Peace broke out in the summer of 1979. In March, the Australian board granted PBL Sports, a Packer subsidiary, exclusive TV rights for ten years. Two months later, PBL Marketing, another Packer tributary, secured a contract to promote Australian cricket for a similar term. WSC promptly disbanded and the ICC readmitted the rebels. Packer had got what he wanted, cricket what it needed. A hefty boot to the vitals.

Match
Highest total: 398 for 5 (Sri Lanka v Kenya, 1996)
Lowest (all out) total: 43 (Pakistan v West Indies, 1993)
Highest individual score: 194 Saeed Anwar (Pakistan v India, 1997)
Best bowling: 7 for 37 Aquib Javed (Pakistan v India, 1991)
Most dismissals by wicketkeeper: 5 – on 18 different occasions
Most catches (fielder): 5 Jonty Rhodes (South Africa v West Indies, 1993)

Inside the Game

One of the more acute brains behind WSC's innovations was Richie Benaud, the ice-cool Australian broadcaster, writer, consultant and erstwhile leg-spinner, not to mention one of the game's most daring and progressive captains. During this period, he lost many friends and admirers. Twenty years later, gravitas long restored, he can be seen as the father-figure of the modern game, respected by most if not quite all. 'Those players and the ones that followed', he once reasoned, 'are earning good money for a combination of good performances and pulling spectators through the turnstile: cricketers in other parts of the world are far better off now than pre-World Series Cricket. There will be some who say that is not a good thing. To that I say ... nonsense.'

Just about everything WSC pioneered is now part of the fixtures and fittings, even motorised drinks carts. The greatest legacy? No contest: night games. At Edgbaston in July 1997, 15,000 men, women and children, three times the average Sunday gathering, turned up on a Wednesday evening to see Warwickshire play Somerset in England's first competitive match under lights; when bad light threatened to stop play in Perth a few months later, floodlights were switched on during a Test for the first time. One day, who knows: the ICC might even get around to filching WSC's second brightest idea: preparing pitches in hothouses, whisking them to grounds by helicopter and dropping them on to the square.

The public clamour for 'instant' or 'pyjama' cricket, as it was dubbed by cynics and purists (usually one and the same), has done more than render Test matches more stimulating. It has also

---

Career
Most appearances: 286 Mohammad Azharuddin (India), Allan Border (Australia)
Most runs: 8,648 Desmond Haynes (West Indies)
Highest average (min. 1,000 runs): 53.20 Michael Bevan (Australia)
Most centuries: 17 Desmond Haynes (West Indies)
Most fifties: 74 Desmond Haynes (West Indies)
Most wickets: 341 Wasim Akram (Pakistan)
Most five-wicket hauls: 9 Waqar Younis (Pakistan)
Most economical bowling (min. 100 overs): 2.85 runs per over Geoff Arnold (England)
Lowest bowling average (min. 100 overs): 17.84 Geoff Arnold (England)
Most dismissals by wicketkeeper: 234 (195 catches, 39 stumpings) Ian Healy (Australia)
Most catches (fielder): 127 Allan Border (Australia)

saved them from extinction. All those Champions Trophies and Singer World Series and Independence Cups may get a mite wearisome, but they fulfil a philanthropic function, underwriting the more aesthetically-pleasing version. The final winter BP (Before Packer) witnessed twenty-two Tests and two one-day internationals; by the time West Indies and Sri Lanka downed swords in mid-June, the 1996–7 southern hemisphere season had encompassed almost a century of one-dayers in addition to thirty-five Tests.

The bee in most bonnets remains the supposed cheapening of the art. In the wake of the 1963 Knockout final, Norman Preston observed with some displeasure that 'the majority of counties were loath to include even one slow bowler and relied mainly on pace', a reservation echoed ever since. Not that this stopped Pakistan's Mushtaq Ahmed, a wrist-spinner incapable of bowling a negative delivery, from deciding the 1992 World Cup final. Nor Shane Warne from becoming Australia's most valued one-day bowler. And what was it that E.W. Swanton opined in 1987? 'The glorification of one-day cricket has led to a disastrous fall in Australian playing standards'? Some disaster.

That said, it would be wrong to suggest that one-day theories have had no impact on the first-class mind. A game in grave danger of dozing off into everlasting sleep has been injected with copious doses of vigour and enterprise. Scoring rates in Tests are much faster, draws well down (or at least boring ones). Improvisation is creeping back (viz. the reverse sweep). Fielding standards have improved beyond all recognition. In a game where grass stains on the knees were once badges of dishonour, laundry bills have gone through the roof. Welcome to the good old days.

THE GREAT MATCH

DAY FIVE (Part One)
Headingley, 21 July 1981

Score at start of play: Australia 401 for 9 declared; England 174 and 351 for 9

For needless nosiness and vigorous vindictiveness the British press may be second to none, but when they make amends they make 'em in style.

For all that his inspirational batting appeared to have done little more than delay the inevitable, the morning papers collectively composed a love song to the man responsible for replenishing English spirits, the same man they had pilloried for the past twelve months. Pat Gibson's report in the Daily Express stretched poetic licence to the brink: 'The amazing Ian Botham had the mourners dancing in the aisles at Headingley last night with the greatest comeback since Lazarus.'

That said, in the cold light of the morning after, the mood was bittersweet. Tony Smith, the Australians' driver and general dogsbody, had already ordered the champagne. Sure enough, any visions of England extending their lead to any meaningful degree evaporated when Alderman had Willis caught by Allan Border with only five runs added and the sun blazing. The final pair had added thirty-seven, runs of inestimable value in such a context; even so, even on this capricious surface, a target of 130 in the best part of six hours looked, if not a doddle, then certainly far from daunting. Not that Brearley could afford to be anything but positive as he addressed his players. 'More aggression', he exhorted, 'more liveliness, more encouragement for the bowlers. They're the ones who are nervous now.'

Brearley faced the captain's most taxing dilemma. With so few runs to play with, the balance between attack and defence could scarcely be more delicate. A collective decision was made to post a third man and a fine leg at all times to prevent any edges or deflections from going for too many runs over the rapid outfield. Reasoning that Dilley and Botham might still have the force with them, Brearley entrusted them with the new ball; although Botham's first two balls were both clattered unceremoniously to the boundary by Graeme Wood, the left-hander from Perth soon misjudged a half-volley from the same golden arm and edged to Bob Taylor behind the stumps. A few minutes previously, while Botham was removing his pads in the dressing-room, Brearley had reminded him of a conversation they had had before the match. 'I had commiserated with him for the way in which he had been harassed and pursued by the media. I had added, half-joking, that he would probably score a century and take twelve wickets. Now, almost a week later, I mentioned that he still owed us six.'

That said, Brearley soon found himself troubled. 'Botham was bowling well, but without sharp movement or real pace. I was more worried about Dilley. His first two overs cost 11 runs. I decided to take him off. He told me he was feeling a thigh strain. For the sixth over I gave the ball to Willis. He said, "Faster and straighter, right?" I nodded.' Brearley was banking on the wind helping Botham's outswing but the ball barely swung in the bright sunshine. Unperturbed, Dyson and Chappell repeated their patient liaison of the first innings, taking the score to fifty-six without further loss or much ado. It was around this time that Willis, who had been singularly unsuccessful huffing and puffing up the slope and into the wind, reiterated a plea he had made to his captain earlier. 'Let me have a go down the wind', he implored, 'I'm an old man now.'

England's senior bowler was exaggerating, albeit barely. Bedevilled by a chest infection at Lord's and a doubtful starter here, Robert George Dylan Willis, 32, had looked positively middle-aged. Despite knocking Hughes's cap off, he had laboured throughout Australia's first innings, wicketless and anxious, his fear of bowling no balls leaving him hesitant. To date, in the second, he had overstepped with unnerving monotony. In the week leading up to the game he had confided in Botham and other close colleagues: he was convinced this would be his last outing for his country. Nor did the gentlemen of the Fourth Estate disagree.

The upshot of Willis's plea, according to Botham, 'was the most magnificent spell of sustained hostile fast bowling it has ever been my privilege to witness'. Chappell was the first victim, parrying a catch to Taylor as a brutish delivery threatened his cherubic features. Then, in the last over before lunch, Willis made two critical incisions, seeing off Hughes and Yallop with balls of equally fiendish bounce. Having swooped low at third slip to catch Hughes, Botham's eyes lit up: 'You could tell something had happened [to them]. As we came out after lunch we looked across the balcony and saw the expression on their faces: talk about rabbits caught in the headlights!'

And there they remained. With the bounce increasingly erratic, batting was now a lottery, and Willis continued to take full advantage. Old interjected to pluck out Border's leg stump via an inside edge (65 for 5) before the Warwickshire man drew Dyson into a mishook that deflected off his gloves and lobbed to Taylor (68 for 6). When Willis lured Marsh into a similar indiscretion, Dilley at long leg completed the catch uneasily, casting around to ascertain whether his feet were inside the boundary: they were, just. A nervy Lawson flailed at a wide one and snicked it to Taylor, who accepted the offering at the second attempt, complete with somersault and toppling sunhat. Shrugging aside his paranoia about overstepping, Willis had taken six wickets for a mere eight runs in six overs; in the first innings he had bowled thirty-seven overs and gone empty-handed. Seventy-five for eight: fifty-five needed and England expectant.

Bright and Lillee, though, were in no mood to go quietly. Taking a leaf out of Botham's book, they opted for boldness, screwing up the tension another few notches. Twice Lillee cut Willis for four; twice Bright pulled

Old for similar reward. In four overs of cool, measured, forthright strokeplay against bowling that was too short too often, the requirement was slashed by thirty-five. The assertive stride of English feet had slowed to a gingery shuffle. Were those peals of laughter coming from the Australian dressing-room, or were the gods themselves sniggering?

THE EMPIRE STRIKES BACK

Packer didn't just turn cricket into a viable product. Unintentional as it may have been, he levelled the playing field. West Indies, Pakistan and New Zealand began beating Australia with worrying frequency; everyone began beating England with worrying frequency.

Once upon a time, you knew where you were with Test cricket. Few were allowed to play it. Newcomers were obliged to endure endless indignities (New Zealand had to wait forty-four games and twenty-four years before recording their first win). White supremacy was seldom challenged. The coloured nations wanted nothing whatsoever to do with South Africa. Not until Packer's intervention did the tide turn in earnest. Sri Lanka waited just four years to break their Test duck, Zimbabwe two. Pakistan emerged from India's shadow. Then, in 1996, Sri Lanka astonished all and sundry by carrying off the World Cup. In the middle of a lengthy and bitter civil war, a national holiday was declared.

Consider the following tables of Test results:

Cricket

MARCH 1877 to OCTOBER 1960

ENGLAND	W	L	D	AUSTRALIA	W	L	D	
v Australia	62	74	42	v England	74	62	42	
v South Africa	45	17	32	v South Africa	27	3	9	
v West Indies	15	10	15	v West Indies	11	2	2	(+ 1 tie)
v New Zealand	11	0	17	v New Zealand	1	0	0	
v India	15	1	8	v India	8	1	4	
v Pakistan	1	1	2	v Pakistan	2	1	1	

OCTOBER 1960 to OCTOBER 1976

ENGLAND	W	L	D	AUSTRALIA	W	L	D
v Australia	9	13	24	v England	13	9	24
v South Africa	1	1	6	v South Africa	2	8	4
v West Indies	6	12	13	v West Indies	13	5	7
v New Zealand	12	0	7	v New Zealand	3	1	2
v India	7	5	12	v India	8	2	2
v Pakistan	8	0	15	v Pakistan	3	0	2

OCTOBER 1976 to 4 MARCH, 1998

ENGLAND	W	L	D	AUSTRALIA	W	L	D	
v Australia	21	27	19	v England	27	21	19	
v South Africa	1	2	5	v South Africa	5	3	4	
v West Indies	7	28	12	v West Indies	11	22	12	
v New Zealand	13	4	14	v New Zealand	12	6	10	
v India	10	8	18	v India	8	6	11	(+ 1 tie)
v Pakistan	5	8	15	v Pakistan	9	10	12	

The second and third tables reveal much. Until Australia's revival in the early 1990s, West Indies and Pakistan had been top dogs for a decade; had Vorster and the Botha Boot Boys not spoiled things, South Africa would undoubtedly have vied for pre-eminence. Having spent much of the 1970s listing badly, HMS England ran aground. In the space of barely six months in 1986, the national team were 'blackwashed' 5–0 in the Caribbean (having been similarly disposed of on home turf two years earlier), then lost successive home series to India and New Zealand, the latter's first such success on English soil. The following winter they regained the Ashes, yet that remains their most recent victory in a five-Test rubber; since then, moreover, their only conquests in a three-Test series have been India and New Zealand.

In March 1998, Australia led the Wisden World Championship (one of seven such blueprints currently being mulled over by the ICC, most of them revolving around an ongoing league rather than a tournament); England ranked seventh. Have the original masters declined or the lower orders simply got uppity? Much as we Poms have a penchant for prolonged navel scrutiny, it seems only right and proper to give credit where it's due.

Which brings us back to Packer. By opening the game up commercially, he alerted players to the possibilities. Overseas stars who would once have been forced to retire at thirty-two or thirty-three in order to secure their futures, are now persisting into their late thirties and early forties, a privilege hitherto reserved almost exclusively for Englishmen, who had always formed the core of the professional game. It was a sign of the times when, in 1997, a dispute over pay saw the leading Australians go to the very brink of a strike.

The first meaningful indication of upheaval came in the winter of 1960–1, when the West Indies and Australia staged a five-course feast for the gods. Hitherto unbeaten in Test rubbers against all but the Poms, the hosts edged home by two wins to one, with two nerve-shredding draws and the circuit's first tie; had the West Indies scored one more run on that historic occasion in Brisbane, and the indomitable gum-chewing Ken Mackay not orchestrated two heroic tail-end rallies, Frank Worrell's men would have prevailed 3–1. As it was, Hall, Griffith, Gibbs, Kanhai and Sobers left an indelible impression. More than 90,000, the largest crowd to date for a single day's play, turned up for the third day of the final Test at Melbourne's cavernous MCG. *Wisden* was left in no doubt about the impact of these so-called 'Calypso' cricketers: 'They revitalised cricket in Australia.'

The key ingredient, none the less, was Worrell's calming, fatherly influence: under his guidance, the Caribbean's representatives had finally found the collective purpose to match their individual gifts. 'You would have to be black, from a colonial background', proposed Michael Manley, the former Jamaican prime minister, 'to understand fully what this meant to the West Indies.'

Before independence, the white ruling classes had dominated the game on the islands, but now a sense of identity had been forged. When bickering forced the West Indian Federation to collapse in the early 1960s, the cricketers were left as the lone standard-bearers for unity. When Australia toured the Caribbean in 1965, Sobers and his cohorts went the whole hog, beating Bob Simpson's men 2–1 after a tempestuous, often brutal struggle. It was official: cricket was no longer a white man's game.

Erraticism set in under Sobers's leadership – the instinctive rarely make good captains – but then came Clive Lloyd. A strong leader with a keen

Master of all: Garfield Sobers

Inside the Game

Black panther: Clive Lloyd

understanding of what cricket could do for black awareness, like Worrell, Lloyd instilled steel. Capitalising on a conveyor belt of lithe, lethal pacemen, he took the unprecedented step of stocking his attack with four genuinely fast bowlers, using spin solely as a means of pepping up the over rate, sending the purists into an almighty froth. And quashing all resistance.

The upshot was the most prolonged period of domination the game has ever known. Between 1980 and 1995, the West Indies did not lose a single series. Between July 1976 and August 1988, they played twenty-seven Tests against England, winning twenty and drawing seven. Between 1979 and 1993, they defeated Australia on sixteen occasions and lost on five. The accountants were not impressed: only rarely, after all, did their matches last beyond the fourth afternoon.

Nor did Lloyd's tactics go down especially well, least of all with those who lacked the ammunition to respond (i.e. the opposition). Granted, there were times when these pace quartets – particularly the trailblazing ensemble of Roberts, Holding, Garner and Croft – did not so much stray over the line as ignore it. The bat became a shield. Even for the tailenders, who, according to the code of the so-called 'fast bowlers' union', were meant to be granted immunity (Lloyd shrewdly insisted his bowlers practised their batting, so they could take it as well as dish it out). Yet the umpires, who were empowered to warn Roberts and Co for intimidation and even ban them from bowling, seldom saw fit to do so.

Something Had To Be Done. So the legislators went to work, imposing a restriction on bouncers.

As it transpired, this proved a far less effective deterrent than the rival attractions of basketball and baseball. And the advent of a man named Shane.

Shane Warne's timing was impeccable. The Caribbean influence had spread like a virus, transforming the game into a celebration of machismo. By the mid-1980s, spin bowling was old hat. The Pakistan leg-break maestro, Abdul Qadir, was alone in commanding a regular place. Though booming at the box-office, cricket was mired in a spiritual slump. Whither subtlety? Whither deception? Tubby, bubbly and drenched in self-belief, Warne brought both back with a vengeance.

It nearly didn't happen. A rebel without pause in his teens and beyond, Warne was the bleach-blond beach boy who had the gall to walk out of the newly-founded Australian Cricket Academy, the elite seat of learning that would do much to pave the way for his country's revival. He was also more accomplished at downing beer than doing push-ups. Fortunately, the time he did spend at the Academy proved fruitful: he discovered how to maintain a respectable level of fitness, met his mentor, Terry Jenner, and, best of all, acquired a flipper. A flipper is a delivery that pitches and skids, a bugger to perfect, even trickier to defy.

Come 1998, Warne had superseded Gibbs' mark of 309 Test wickets, the most by a slow bowler. That he was still in his twenties was more remarkable still, scuppering a number of well-oiled theories. Ambling in to bowl as they generally do, spinners can carry on playing at a high level deep into their forties; they're not even supposed to be in their prime until their early thirties.

Wristy business: Shane Warne

Inside the Game

This time the virus was more benign. For a team to include two 'twirlers' – once the norm – is no longer regarded as a sign of complete and utter dottiness. India, Pakistan, South Africa, Zimbabwe and Sri Lanka all field leg-spinners, not as a fashion statement but in recognition of a vital weapon. Courtesy of Pakistan's precocious Saqlain Mushtaq, even off-spin is becoming sexy again.

In 1930, Arthur Mailey, the great Australian leg-spinner, was reprimanded for giving advice to his young English counterpart, Ian Peebles. He was aghast. 'Slow bowling is an art, Mr Kelly', he brusquely informed the official concerned, 'and art is international.' Sixty years on, Warne went to Abdul Qadir's home and was given a masterclass on the lounge rug.

Bobby Simpson, once Australia's national coach, is now a consultant to India. Bob Woolmer, once of Kent and England, coaches South Africa. So perhaps we should not make too much of cricket's debt to patriotism. Besides, it's not as if the players are inflexible in their loyalties. Fourteen have represented two nations, the first and most notorious Billy Midwinter, the only man to play both for England against Australia in Australia and for Australia against England in England. The tug of war was most unseemly.

Having emigrated Down Under, the Gloucestershire-born Midwinter turned out for Australia in the inaugural Test, taking five for seventy-eight. While touring England the following year, he was kidnapped from the Lord's dressing-room by good ol' WG, who duly bundled him into a taxi and hustled him off to the Oval to play for Gloucestershire. Midwinter remained with his native county for the remainder of the summer, toured Australia with Alfred Shaw's side in 1881-2, then declared himself 'an Australian to the heart's core'; the next winter he played in the final Test *against* England. Long neglected, his Melbourne grave was restored by the Australian Cricket Society in the late 1970s.

A century later came the hullaballoo over the Hollioake brothers. If there was ever a sign of English despair, it was surely the part played by a Prime Minister in ensuring these gifted young Australians qualified to defend the realm rather than attack it. John Major, a lifelong Surrey fan, helped hurry through the appropriate papers registering them as English for cricketing purposes, even though Adam had already played for the Australian youth team. When he and his prodigious younger brother Ben played together in the one-day international against Australia at Lord's in 1997, their ears were left burning by a barrage of decidedly unsweet nothings from their erstwhile countrymen. Many Englishmen were equally offended when Adam was appointed captain of the one-day side for the Champions Trophy in Sharjah. The blighter even had the barefaced effrontery to lead them to victory.

United: Ben and Adam Hollioake

It was an important triumph, for the greater good as much as the winners. Sure, the game's power base lies in India, Australia and South Africa. Sure, the future lies in south-east Asia. But cricket urgently needs a tad more starch in those slack upper lips.

England may have laid the egg that hatched the golden goose but they have never won the World Cup: rectifying that in front of their countrymen in 1999 would be timely indeed. All the same, it is in the longer form of the game, the one the players themselves regard as the ultimate challenge, that progress is most imperative. Mark Taylor, Australia's worldly-wise captain, was not being diplomatic when he remarked that the survival of the Test match depends on it.

England is the only country on the Test circuit where houses are packed regardless of how the home team are faring (and not only because none of the grounds holds more than 30,000). Tests here are still social occasions, the result secondary. It is also the only country that still stages more Tests in a season than close encounters of the biff-bang variety. Elsewhere, five-day attendances are falling, pyjama parties all the rage. Can a generation of Poms weaned on failure and humiliation maintain the enthusiasm of their forebears without the occasional soupçon of encouragement? Doubtful.

The problem is that the professional game in England is still run by the eighteen county clubs, who would all be out of business but for the gate receipts and TV millions engendered by international fixtures. Gratitude, sadly, is in short supply. Such is their single-minded self-interest and tireless short-termism, the counties can be relied upon to promote mediocrity and ensure few of the obvious steps are taken.

County cricket, indeed, can be seen as a throwback to Feudalism. Players are permitted to change counties only under certain restrictive circumstances (the European Union is currently deliberating over whether this amounts to restraint of trade). In contrast to any other major team sport, there is no transfer or trade system. To encourage loyalty, players are offered a carrot known as 'the benefit': after ten years' service, provided they've tugged forelock with sufficient gusto, they are entitled to spend a season raising funds from supporters and well-wishers, caps firmly in hand.

More energy is expended preserving than progressing. It took the best part of twenty years for floodlights to catch on. Oxford and Cambridge, for whom even victories over understrength county XIs are extremely unusual, are still deemed worthy of first-class status. Then again, what else can one expect of a land where yesterday means more than tomorrow?

As 1997 dawned, hope sprang anew. The ECB had taken over from the TCCB and structural change was top of the agenda. Chairman Lord MacLaurin vowed that 'no change was not an option', getting his members' backs up from the outset. Mark Butcher, fresh from a successful tour of Australia with the England A team, was more enthusiastic. 'Whenever I go anywhere, all people do is say English cricket is no good. It hurts. You try to defend it but there isn't a great deal to defend. Which is why I don't bother any more. What's required is something absolutely drastic. It's going to hurt some people but if we want a successful England team, sacrifices must be made. The only thing I can envisage making any significant difference is to lose ten counties and pool the players among the rest. But it'll never happen.'

In terms of fulfilling the main objectives – heightened competitiveness and a less debilitating fixture list – the rational alternative, even a few hard-bitten traditionalists acknowledged, was to split the championship into two divisions. This could be done on a parallel, regional basis (which would certainly ease the burden of those interminable motorway hikes) or, better still, incorporate the cut and thrust of promotion and relegation. While the latter option was welcomed by the well-off (i.e. those clubs attached to the six designated Test grounds), the lesser-heeled recoiled in fear. Who'd want to play for (let alone watch) a second division team? The nays had it.

Before votes were cast, the *Daily Telegraph* expressed an even graver concern. It came from the typewriter of the paper's erstwhile cricket correspondent, the venerable E.W. 'Jim' Swanton, acclaimed as 'the doyen' in the *Oxford Dictionary of World Cricketers* (a seemingly all-encompassing labour of love whose 800-odd pages contrive to include entries on umpires, commentators and even women while excluding Kerry Packer, airbrushing the lout from history). Promotion and relegation? Jim could imagine nothing more damaging. Heavens, he spluttered, it might make the players '*too* competitive'.

THE GREAT MATCH

DAY FIVE (Part Two)
Headingley, 21 July 1981

The last thing Brearley wanted to do was take the ball away from Willis. He realised, none the less, that the tiring bowler could do with some encouragement. Trouble was, his mind was a blank. Thickset and thrustful, Gatting bustled over. 'Tell Bob to just bowl straight at Dennis', he advised as his Middlesex colleague headed in Willis's direction. 'It doesn't matter much what length.' Brearley, to whom this had occured, concurred and passed on the message. Four balls later, Lillee scooped a full delivery from Willis towards mid-on and who should complete the execution but Gatting. He only just made it, mind. Darting forward, he lost his footing and had to fling himself full-length to get his fingers under the ball and did so milliseconds before it hit the turf. As he thudded to earth, right hand aloft, the ground seemed to shake. Willis just about had the strength to clench a fist.

Recalling Botham in place of Old, Brearley spread his field deep to allow Bright to take a single early in the over, hoping to attack the more vulnerable Alderman; Bright duly obliged. Asked by Brearley whether he would prefer a third slip or a gully, Botham opted for the former, only to look on aghast as Old dropped Alderman twice in three balls in that very position. 'Perhaps it was as well', reflected Brearley, 'that it was a Yorkshireman standing [there].'

Insidethe**Game**

Willis, though, was not to be denied. Hair streaming, elbows pumping, knees pounding, he scampered in for the first ball of the following over and unleashed an inch-perfect yorker; beaten for pace, Bright drove over it and heard the death-rattle as his leg stump turned cartwheels. On poured the crowd as the players sought souvenir stumps or anything else that would serve as a memento. At 2.20 p.m., with the result in doubt to the very last after the equivalent of eighteen back-to-back football matches, England had won by eighteen runs. Alfred Hitchcock gazed down wistfully from his cloud, wishing he could have plotted anything half as suspenseful.

Eyes aglaze with the intensity of it all, Willis sprinted for the pavilion. When interviewed a few minutes later he appeared to be in an advanced state of shock. So deeply had he immersed himself in what he called his 'cocoon of concentration', he made little or no sense, choosing to chide the media. Only when he turned on his car radio three hours later did he emerge from his trance. 'Not until Henry Blofeld's fruity tones regaled me with the details of the Test did I realise what had actually happened: it was me he was talking about. I had taken 8 for 43. It slowly dawned on me that I had played my full part in the most astonishing few hours of cricket I had known.'

The Man of the Match award, none the less, went to Botham, and rightly so. Without his derring-do the previous afternoon, Willis would never have had anything to bowl at. The adjudicator, Fred Trueman, an ancient master with a marked tendency to sneer at all things modern, acclaimed Botham's match haul of 7 wickets and 199 runs as 'the greatest all-round performance I've ever seen in a Test'. And then, just to rub it in: 'A captain's performance that came one match too late.'

The Stock Exchange closed early. In the Commons, MPs paused to salute Botham and his accomplices. Desperate for the vaguest sign of cheer amid a summer of street riots and rampant discontent, BBC TV and radio both led their evening bulletins with the saga of England's historic triumph. Only a few thousand had born witness in person – the total attendance was 52,566 – but the invisible audience of millions, rooted to TVs, trannies and telephones in homes, offices and factories from Blackburn to Whitehall, had had their nerves chopped, fried, grilled and roasted.

For all their captain's graciousness, the Australians were inconsolable. And scars remain. On the same ground sixteen summers later, while the giant video screen was showing highlights of the match as a welcome diversion during a rain interruption, Lawson grimaced as he saw himself bowling to Botham on that fateful Monday. 'Look at all those slips', he cried. 'All his edges were going over their heads. What were we thinking of?'

Lawson recalled how, when the England dressing-room attendant was dispatched to the visitors' dressing-room to request a loan of some of that unpopped bubbly, the

Inside the Game

poor chap was sent on his way with an earful of fleas. Lillee and Marsh laid their winnings on the table with a suitably apologetic air. That the side's fiercest competitors had backed the opposition provoked not so much as a single quizzical look or accusing editorial.

Baffled by the behaviour of his pitch, Keith Boyce, the Headingley groundsman, sent a sample to the Soil Research Centre for analysis. 'A portion should have been consigned to the Department of Information', reasoned the editor of 'Wisden Cricket Monthly', David Frith, 'as a symbol and reminder of the fighting spirit which not only won a famous Test but can win much larger social and economic battles.' I'm always reminded of something Tommy Judd said to Guy Bennett in Julian Mitchell's 'Another Country'. 'You know what I really hate about cricket', revealed Tommy as the pair watched a match at Eton. 'It's such a damn good game.'

Just the job, Bob: Willis strikes again, inspiring England to the most improbable Test victory of all

DREAM TEAMS — Cricket

[Key: RHB Right-hand batsman; LHB Left-hand batsman; RF/RFM/RM Right-arm fast/fast-medium/medium-pace bowler; LF/LFM Left-arm fast/fast-medium; OS Off-spinner; SLA Slow left-arm; WS Wrist-spinner; WKT Wicketkeeper]

PAST MASTERS XI

Sunil Gavaskar (Bombay, Somerset & India)
RHB b Bombay, 1949

Nobody defied the Caribbean pace barrage with greater resolution. Compact, composed and correct, the first man to score 10,000 Test runs started as he meant to go on: his maiden series (v West Indies, 1970–1) saw him become the first to collect a double-century and a century in the same Test. His thirteen three-figure scores against the West Indies were more than twice as many as any peer; pride of place went to his 102 in Trinidad (1976), when he guided India to 406 for 4, the highest fourth-innings total to win a Test.

Vital statistics: 125 Tests; 10,122 runs (average 51.12); 34 centuries; Best: 236

Soundest bite: 'This was not great captaincy, it was barbarism' (on Clive Lloyd's handling of the West Indies attack).

Sir Len Hutton (Yorkshire & England)
RHB b Pudsey, Yorkshire, 1916–90

Dour, dedicated and uncompromising, England's first professional captain was the hero the nation craved in the decade after the Second World War; no mean feat given that a gym accident had left one arm shorter than the other. At 21, he relieved Bradman of the world Test record with 364 against Australia (1938) but it was stoicism in the face of the searing pace of Ray Lindwall and Keith Miller that made him a national monument. That and the fact that in 1953, after twenty fallow years, England regained the Ashes under his command.

Vital statistics: 79 Tests; 6,971 runs at 56.67; 19 centuries; Best: 364

Soundest bite: 'His bat was part of his nervous system' (Harold Pinter).

Sir Donald Bradman (South Australia, New South Wales & Australia)
RHB b Cootamundra, New South Wales, 1908

The irresistible force who never acknowledged an immoveable object. Slightly-built, quick-witted and even quicker-footed, he bore the burden of a young nation's aspirations with remarkable fortitude, not least when 'Bodyline' was devised to curb him. 'What makes you think I would only have maintained it?' he replied indignantly upon being advised that he would have doubled Gavaskar's run-tally had he kept up his 99.94 average for 125 Tests. 'If I'd had the opportunity to play in India, Pakistan and Sri Lanka, I think I would have increased it.'

Vital statistics: 52 Tests; 6,996 runs at 99.94; 29 centuries; Best: 334

Soundest bite: 'No one ever laughed about Bradman. He was no laughing matter' (R.C. Robertson-Glasgow).

Viv Richards (Antigua, Somerset, Glamorgan & West Indies)
RHB b Antigua, 1952

Here was black power in the most literal sense. Inspired by a combustible mix of pride and prejudice, he derived his 'Smokin' Joe' nickname from his resemblance to the boxer Joe Frazier, and stirred only marginally less fear, notably among opponents of English extraction. After leading Somerset to the first trophies in their history, he pillaged his county chums for the fastest-ever century in Tests (56 balls, 1986), yet left even more mouths agape with the inventive savagery that won the 1979 World Cup final.

Soundest bite: 'Truly, I think I could get more runs if England had some faster bowlers.'

George Headley (Jamaica & West Indies) RHB b Panama, 1909–83

The Horatio of the Sward: no batsman has stood so alone so defiantly so often. Vastly stronger than his spare frame suggested, the original masterblaster gave up his dentistry studies in the US to play in the West Indies' inaugural Test (1930), and scored 176. Such was his dominance, one three-year period saw him post nine centuries to his colleagues' one. One of only four batsmen to average 60-plus in Tests, he was also the West Indies' first black captain. Adoring Jamaicans dubbed Bradman 'the white Headley'.

Vital statistics: 19 Tests; 2,190 runs at 60.82; 10 centuries; Best: 270

Soundest bite: 'They could sit in the same cathedral as George but not in the same pew' (Berkeley Gaskin comparing him to his Caribbean successors).

Sir Gary Sobers (Barbados, South Australia, Nottinghamshire & West Indies) LHB, RFM, SLA, WS b 1936, Bridgetown, Barbados

Born with five fingers on either hand, and the phenomena just kept coming. The world's premier batsman for many years (his 365 against Pakistan in 1957–8 survived as a Test peak for the best part of four decades), he was also four bowlers in one – pace, swing and two brands of spin – as well as a brilliant fielder. After enduring his unprecedented six sixes in an over for Nottinghamshire (1968), the Glamorgan captain Tony Lewis spoke of 'scientific hitting with every movement working in harmony'; the one thing he didn't detect was sweat. In 1997, he won £200,000 in the Barbados Lottery.

Vital statistics: 93 Tests; 8,032 runs at 57.78; 26 centuries; Best: 365 not out Bowling: 235 wickets at 34.03; Five wickets in inns: 6; Best 6–73

Soundest bite: 'He was prepared to stand or fall by his belief that cricket, even at Test level, should be entertaining' (Ray Illingworth).

Ian Botham (Somerset, Worcestershire, Durham, Queensland & England) RHB LFM b Heswall, Cheshire, 1955

Grabbed life by the balls, gave them a vigorous shake and never let go. For a few years he even rivalled Sobers for all-round par excellence: no player has dominated a Test the way he did against India in 1980, following a century with thirteen wickets, but then single-handed victories were his stock-in-trade. 'He's Biggles, the VC, El Alamein', claimed his agent. 'How could any schoolboy not want to be Ian Botham?' In his fearsome, fearless, often feckless pomp, few English schoolboys, at least, were prepared to differ.

Vital statistics: 102 Tests; 5,200 runs at 33.54; 14 centuries; Best: 208 Bowling: 383 wkts at 28.40; Five wkts/inns; 27; 10 wkts/match: 4; Best: 8–34

Soundest bite: 'The first rock'n'roll cricketer' (Len Hutton).

Alan Knott (Kent & England) RHB WKT b Belvedere, Kent, 1946

Fanatically fit and astonishingly agile, feisty with the bat and fastidious to a fault, he set fresh standards for what the world expected of a wicketkeeper. As deft standing back to pace as crouching to spin, this 1970s cult figure struck up an almost telepathic relationship with his Kent confrere, Derek Underwood, en route to outstripping another Canterbury titan, Godfrey Evans, as England's finest gloveman. Distinguished by their impish, unorthodox and determined style, the runs were an unnecessary if welcome bonus.

Vital statistics: 95 Tests; 4,389 runs at 32.75; five centuries; Best: 135; 250 catches + 19 stumpings

Soundest bite: 'I have played my best cricket when I have been with my wife.'

Dennis Lillee (Western Australia, Northamptonshire & Australia) RF b Perth, Western Australia, 1949

Courage, bluff and unbridled competitiveness were the hallmarks of Australia's foremost fast bowler. After terrorising England in 1972, he broke down with stress fractures of the back, an injury that would have finished many a lesser man, yet returned better – and shrewder – than ever. Not that he had mislaid that vicious streak: Viv Richards

insists his chief inspiration was the pummelling he and the West Indies batsmen suffered in the winter of 1975–6. Behind that malevolent moustache lay a master craftsman and shameless showman.

Vital statistics: 70 Tests; 355 wickets at 23.92; 5 wkts/inns: 23; 10 wkts/match: 7

Soundest bite: 'There's no batsman on earth who goes out to meet him with a smile' (Clive Lloyd).

Bill O'Reilly (New South Wales & Australia) WS b White Cliffs, New South Wales, 1905-96

As belligerent in the field as he would later prove in print (he retired to the press box), here was a leg-spinner blessed with a fast bowler's fire and rage. Confounding his breed's traditions for patience, he bowled with relentless hostility, the action a blur of arms and legs, the results bamboozling. No respecter of reputations, he was constantly at loggerheads with Bradman, openly cheering when his countryman was dismissed for a duck in his final Test. Bradman still said he was the best bowler he ever faced.

Vital statistics: 27 Tests; 144 wickets at 22.59;

Best 7–54; 5 wkts/inns: 11; 10 wkts/match: 3

Soundest bite: 'To hit him for four ... was almost like disturbing a hive of bees. He seemed to attack from all directions' (Bradman).

Sydney Barnes (Warwickshire, Lancashire, Staffordshire & England) RM, WS b Smethwick, Staffordshire, 1873–1967

Generation after generation have taken it on blind trust that the world has never seen a deadlier bowler. Perfecting the fast leg-break, he bemused with swerve, cut, flight and variations of pace, averaging an astonishing seven victims per Test; 49 wickets in four games against South Africa in 1913–14, still a record for a Test series, helped him go out with a resounding bang – at 40. At 80 he took the first over of his benefit match, but declined the new ball, claiming he 'didn't want to get the game over with too quickly'.

Vital statistics: 189 wickets at 16.43; Best: 9–103; 5 wkts/inns: 24; 10 wkts/match: 7

Soundest bite: 'No bugger ever got all ten when I was at the other end' (on Jim Laker's 10–53 against Australia).

Cricket

165

Inside the Game

NEW WORLD ORDER XI

Mark Taylor (New South Wales & Australia, captain)
LHB b Wagga Wagga, New South Wales, 1964

Australia owes plenty to his resourceful batting and prehensile slip-catching, even more to his perceptive, imaginative leadership and man-management skills. By February 1998 he had presided over nine victorious series in a row. A disciplined opener whose 839 runs in the 1989 Ashes series rank second only to Bradman among Australians, his century against England at Edgbaston in 1997, albeit in defeat, was one of the most heroic of the modern era. After 20 innings without a 50, failure would have spelt sayonara; it was testimony to his captaincy that he hadn't gone long before. His wife bet on him to break his drought at 25–1 and won £250.

Sayanath Jayasuriya (Bloomfield & Sri Lanka)
LHB SLA b Matara, 1969

No opener has more strongly refuted the notion that patience and enterprise are mutually exclusive. In 1992, this petite figure gave a hint of his power and audacity by lofting the very first ball he received in a Test for six, completing Sri Lanka's first win over England. Enchanting crowds throughout the Indian subcontinent, he was the star of the 1996 World Cup, and set a record for the fastest one-day international century. Then, in 1997, he threatened Lara's 375 with 340 against India, sharing in a Test-record stand of 576 with Roshan Mahanama as Sri Lanka amassed an unprecedented 952 for six. A new breed.

Brian Lara (Trinidad and Tobago, Warwickshire & West Indies)
LHB b Santa Cruz, Trinidad, 1969

The outstanding batsman of the age, and the finest left-hander since Sobers. Within six weeks in 1994 he scaled the twin peaks: 375 (v England) to smash Sobers's 36-year-old Test record, then, 501 (for Warwickshire) to erase Hanif Mohammad's 35-year-old first-class mark (and inspire a brand of jeans); not for 60 years had both been the property of one man. More awesome still was his 180 (out of 219) against Jamaica earlier that year, 131 of which came while 12 were being scored at the other end. 'He reduced the game to farce', insisted chairman of selectors David Holford. Good thing he discovered mortality.

Sachin Tendulkar (Bombay, Yorkshire & India)
RHB RM OS b Bombay, 1973

If Lara is Beethoven, meet Mozart. A child prodigy, he scored his first 100 for his school at 12, hit successive triple-centuries at 14, made an unbeaten 100 on his first-class debut at 15, and collected his maiden Test century at 17: too young to drive, let alone sign his tour contract, yet old enough to save his country. Before long he couldn't leave his home without being mobbed; unlike so many, he retained focus. Technically sounder than Lara, and less easily bored, he has maintained greater consistency without quite attaining the same heights. As yet. Losing the Indian captaincy may prove a blessing.

Graham Thorpe (Surrey & England)
LHB b Farnham, Surrey, 1969

The silent wind in HMS England's sails. For much of his career a diamond surrounded by mere stones, his unassuming, undemonstrative approach belies the inventiveness and aggression of his strokeplay. Those who

166

Cricket

espy worth only in statistical terms might cite a comparative scarcity of substantial scores as a significant flaw, but the impetus this slight, jaunty figure has given to an innings, daring to attack from the stickiest of predicaments, makes such considerations largely irrelevant. Proud possessor of the most sublime cover drive in Europe.

Steve Waugh (New South Wales, Somerset & Australia)
RHB RM b Sydney, 1965

For incontrovertible proof that cricket is played in the mind, look no further. In his first 42 Test innings, the elder of the prolific Waugh twins failed to score a century (but for his useful seamers he might have been discarded for good); since breaking his duck in 1989, however, the game has known no more dependable run-getter. Eschewing the extravagance of youth, rigorous concentration became his trademark, the innings that decided rubbers against West Indies (1995) and England (1997) a triumph for sheer will. Asked to describe himself, the reply condemned those with greater gifts: 'Someone who makes the most of his ability.'

Ian Healy (Queensland & Australia)
RHB WKT b Spring Hill, Queensland, 1964

Hugely committed, highly charged and as loathed by opponents as he is loved by colleagues. All you really need to know about this puckish character is that by the time he became the first wicketkeeper to appear in 100 Tests, he had never been dropped and had missed just one game through injury. His deftness and agility behind the stumps contrasts with the ungainly obduracy of his batting, his speciality the lost cause. '[He] has only ever seen Australia's cause', wrote Peter Roebuck, the former Somerset captain, 'and he throws himself into it as a hungry dog throws itself upon a corpse.'

Wasim Akram (Lahore, Pakistan Automobile Corporation, Lancashire & Pakistan)
LHB LF b Lahore, 1966

A vibrant heir to a thorny throne. Set the unenviable task of following the all-round colossi of the 1970s and 1980s, no one can fault him for effort: with more than 300 wickets and 2,000 runs in Tests, only Botham, Imran, Hadlee and Kapil can match him. Arguably the most rapid left-armer of all, the source of his crowning glory was that audacious blade. Against Zimbabwe in 1997 he made 257 not out, the highest in Tests by a No.8, orchestrating an eight-wicket stand of 313 that eclipsed the 66-year-old record by the little matter of 67 runs. Never knowingly daunted.

Shane Warne (Victoria & Australia) WS b Ferntree Gully, 1969

Just call him Merlin. Tests were being played out against a backdrop of endles space and splintering bones until, with one delivery to Mike Gatting at Old Trafford in 1993, this brash young man transformed all. Pitched outside leg stump, it spun 18 inches, darted behind the awestruck batsman's legs and struck off-stump; suddenly, after 30 years in the doldrums, wrist spin was sexy again. Though blighted by finger and shoulder problems, he remains on course to be the first to 500 Test scalps. Like Botham, noted Steve Waugh, he possesses 'that rare and special ability to conjure something from nothing'.

Mushtaq Ahmed (Multan, United Bank, Somerset & Pakistan)
WS b Sahiwal, 1970

Where Warne weaves his spells with an insouciance bordering on diffidence, his chief rival in artful dodgerness bounces and bubbles. Warne gave him some handy tips about containment but he still prefers to outwit than wear down; reading his googly is like trying to crack some extra terrestrial code. Yet for all that old-fashioned willingness to trade runs for wickets, he is equally effective in the shorter game, as testified by three critical English wickets in the 1992 World Cup final. Described as 'a model overseas player' by the Somerset cricket chairman, Brian Rose, his zest for his trade is unquenchable.

Glenn McGrath (New South Wales & Australia) RF b Dubbo, New South Wales, 1970

Lean and mean, straight-backed and strident, he was unquestionably the game's most potent purveyor of pace when back trouble beset him in late 1997. And never more vividly than against Lara in 1995–6: cramping him with metronomic accuracy and frustrating him to the point of self-destruction, he dismissed him five times in the first six innings of the series, for 26, 1, 2, 2 and 2, effectively breaking the opposition's spirit. Steve Waugh likened his destruction of England at Lord's in 1997 – when he took 8–38, the best-ever analysis by an Australian at HQ – to 'a dental surgeon working on decayed teeth'.

Cricket

BE AN INSTANT BLUFFER

Want to impress your family/friends/boss with your vast knowledge of all things flanneled and foolish without shelling out the equivalent of the GNP of Burkina Faso on reference works and videos? The following Top Tens should do nicely.

Trailblazers

Kerry Packer
Basil D'Oliveira
Shane Warne
John Nyren
W.G. Grace
Frank Worrell
Don Bradman
Pelham Warner
Ali Bacher
Derek Birley

Time Capsule (matches)

Australia v West Indies, Brisbane, 1960
Australia v West Indies, Adelaide, 1961
Australia v West Indies, Adelaide, 1993
England v Australia, the Oval, 1902
England v West Indies, Lord's, 1963
England v Australia, Manchester, 1961
India v Australia, Madras, 1986
Warwickshire v Hampshire, Edgbaston, 1922
Australia v West Indies, Mohali, 1996 (World Cup semi-final)
West Indies v England, Port of Spain, 1998

Time Capsule (teams)

West Indies 1980–8
Australia 1946–51
England 1953–8
Australia 1994–8
West Indies 1963–6
South Africa 1965–70
Australia 1920–5
England 1886–90
West Indies 1975–9 (limited overs)
Sri Lanka 1996–7 (limited overs)

Time Capsule (feats)

Laker's 19 wickets at Old Trafford (1956)
Bradman's 300 in a day at Headingley (1930)
Botham's 118 at Old Trafford (1981)
Jessop's 104 at the Oval (1902)
Hunte's throw at Brisbane (1961)
Bond's catch at Lord's (1971 Gillette Cup final)
Steve Waugh's 200 at Sabina Park (1995)
Kapil Dev's four successive sixes at Lord's (1990)
India's 406 for four at Port of Spain (1976)
Richards's final blow at Lord's (1979 World Cup final)

Artistic Impression (batsmen)

David Gower (England)
Mohammad Azharuddin (India)
Tom Graveney (England)
Mark Waugh (Australia)
Greg Chappell (Australia)
Jeff Dujon (West Indies)
Zaheer Abbas (Pakistan)
Brian Lara (West Indies)
Barry Richards (South Africa)
Frank Woolley (England)

Artistic Impression (bowlers)

Bishen Bedi (India)
Michael Holding (West Indies)
Jeff Thomson (Australia)
Keith Miller (Australia)
Intikhab Alam (Pakistan)
Phil Tufnell (England)
Graham McKenzie (Australia)
Hedley Howarth (New Zealand)
Garfield Sobers (West Indies: allegro)
Garfield Sobers (West Indies: andante)

Heavy Hitters

Viv Richards (West Indies)
Ian Botham (England)
Gilbert Jessop (England)
Sayanath Jayasuriya (Sri Lanka)
Arthur Wellard (England)
Kapil Dev (India)
Gordon Greenidge (West Indies)
Alistair Brown (England)
Everton Weekes (West Indies)
Edward Alletson (Kent)

Dramatic Appealers

Dennis Lillee (Australia)
Dominic Cork (England)
Abdul Qadir (Pakistan)
Mushtaq Ahmed (Pakistan)
Shane Warne (Australia)
Craig McDermott

Insidethe Game

(Australia)
Richard Hadlee (New Zealand)
Fred Trueman (England)
Curtly Ambrose (West Indies)
Richie Benaud (Australia)

Dastardly Duos (bowlers)

Lillee & Thomson (Australia)
Grimmett & O'Reilly (Australia)
Walsh & Ambrose (West Indies)
Lindwall & Miller (Australia)
Wasim & Waqar (Pakistan)
Roberts and Holding (West Indies)
Trueman & Statham (England)
Marshall & Ambrose (West Indies)
Lock & Laker (England)
Bedi & Chandrasekhar (India)

Dastardly Duos (batsmen)

Greenidge & Haynes (West Indies)
Hobbs & Sutcliffe (England)
Bradman & Ponsford (Australia)
Tendulkar & Azharuddin (India)
Walcott & Weekes (West Indies)
Sobers & Kanhai (West Indies)
Simpson & Lawry (Australia)
Hutton & Washbrook (England)

Boycott & Edrich (England)
Mohsin & Mudassar (Pakistan)

Handy Hands (close fielders)

Roger Harper (West Indies)
Mark Taylor (Australia)
Bobby Simpson (Australia)
Mark Waugh (Australia)
Phil Sharpe (England)
Greg Chappell (Australia)
Walter Hammond (England)
Colin Cowdrey (England)
Garfield Sobers (West Indies)
Nasser Hussain (England)

Fleet Feet (outfielders)

Jonty Rhodes (South Africa)
Derek Randall (England)
Colin Bland (South Africa)
Clive Lloyd (West Indies)
Ross Edwards (Australia)
Gilbert Jessop (England)
Learie Constantine (West Indies)
Paul Sheahan (Australia)
Ricky Ponting (Australia)
Herschelle Gibbs (South Africa)

Most Fiendish Facial Hair

W.G. Grace (England)
Fred 'The Demon' Spofforth (Australia)
Dennis Lillee (Australia)
Joe Darling (Australia)
Stanley Jackson (England)
Percy Sherwell (South Africa)
Reggie Spooner (England)

Syd 'Tich' Gregory (Australia)
Ernie Jones (Australia)
Merv Hughes (Australia)

Sex Objects

Imran Khan (Pakistan)
Sachin Tendulkar (India)
Keith Miller (Australia)
Kapil Dev (India)
Brian Lara (West Indies)
Denis Compton (England)
Dennis Lillee (Australia)
Nick Knight (England)
David Hookes (Australia)
Ted Dexter (England)

World Select XI 2005

Matthew Elliott (Australia)
Saurav Ganguly (India)
Mark Ramprakash (England, captain)
Azhar Mahmood (Pakistan)
Ricky Ponting (Australia)
Mohammad Wasim (Pakistan)
Ben Hollioake (England)
Mark Boucher (South Africa, wicketkeeper)
Nixon McLean (West Indies)
Makhaya Ntini (South Africa)
Chris Schofield (England)

Crunchiest Numbers

394,000 (Estimated five-day crowd at Calcutta, India v England, 1982)
196,754 (copies of umpire Dickie Bird's autobiography sold to 8 March 1998)
2,218 (wickets taken by

Cricket

Glamorgan's Don Shepherd, never capped by England)
281 (Test career bowling average of England's John Warr)
99.7 (fastest recorded delivery – mph – by Jeff Thomson,1975)
72 (age of oldest first-class cricketer, Raja Maharaj Singh, Governor of Bombay)
28 (Test ducks suffered by West Indies' Courtney Walsh)
11 (reputed age of youngest first-class cricketer, Esmail Ahmed Baporia, India)
4.37 (Test career batting average of India's Bhagwat Chandrasekhar)
0 (Number of times England have beaten Australia in a Lord's Test since 1934)

Writers/Journalists

Matthew Engel
Derek Birley
Ray Robinson
C.L.R. James
Jack Fingleton
David Foot
Neville Cardus
Mike Marqusee
Scyld Berry
Christopher Martin-Jenkins

Books

The Pageant of Cricket by David Frith
The Willow Wand by Derek Birley
Beyond A Boundary by C.L.R. James
On Top Down Under by Ray Robinson
Walter Hammond – The Reasons Why by David Foot
The Art of Captaincy by Mike Brearley
Benaud on Reflection by Richie Benaud
Anyone But England by Mike Marqusee
The History of Cricket from the Weald to the Wold by Peter Wynne-Thomas
A Lot of Hard Yakka by Simon Hughes

Verse Or Worse

'The Catch' by Alfred Cochrane
'How Plaxtol Beat Roughway' by Albert Kinross
'Ninth Wicket' by A.P. Herbert
'Epitaph' by George McWilliam
'An Englishman's Crease' by Hubert Phillips
'The Extra Inch' by Siegfried Sassoon
'Watching Benaud Bowl' by Alan Ross
'The Church Cricketant' by Norman Gale
'Cricket at Harrow' by Lord Byron
'The Song of Tilly Lally' by William Blake

Commentators (TV & Radio)

Richie Benaud
John Arlott
Alan McGilvray
'Reds' Perreira
Mark Nicholas
Michael Holding
Christopher Martin-Jenkins
Neville Oliver
Tony Cozier
Brian Johnston

Magazines/Websites/Videos

Wisden Cricket Monthly (magazine)
Inside Edge (magazine)
Cricket Digest (magazine)
'The Tied Test' (video)
'Cricket: The 70s' (video)
'Botham's Ashes' (video)
'Cricketing Legends: Donald Bradman' (video)
'Cricketing Legends: Ray Illingworth' (video)
Benson & Hedges Golden Greats-Batsmen (video)
'CricInfo' (website)

Songs with Cricket References

'When An Old Cricketer Leaves the Crease' (Roy Harper)
'I'm A Boy' (The Who)
'Howzat' (Sherbert)
'Dreadlock Holiday' (10cc)
'Here Come The Aussies' (1972 Australian Ashes Tour Squad)
'The Kerry Packer Song' (John Dengate)
'Bradman' (Paul Kelly)
'The Tiger and the Don' (Ted Egan)
'Our Don Bradman' (Art Leonard)
'I Scored a Hundred in the Backyard at Mum's' (Greg Champion)

ABOUT THE AUTHOR

Rob Steen is an award-winning sportswriter and author currently covering cricket for *The Guardian*, the *Sunday Telegraph*, the *Financial Times* and *Wisden Cricket Monthly*. He has also made many appearances on radio and TV, and is the editor of *The New Ball*, a forthcoming book of new cricket writing.

His previous books include *Spring, Summer, Autumn* (*Guardian* Sports Book of the Year), *Sonny Boy – The Life and Strife of Sonny Liston* ('one of the best boxing books from a British writer for many years' – *The Times*), *Britannic Assurance Guide to County Cricket*, *Desmond Haynes – Lion of Barbados*, *The Mavericks – English Football When Flair wore Flares* ('A lovely read' – *Irish Post*), *David Gower – A Man out of Time* and *Poms and Cobbers* ('A gifted and worldly writer' – Matthew Engel).

Hailed by *Time Out* as 'one of the finest sportswriters in the country', he wears his forty years better than he feared.

ABOUT THE SERIES

InsidetheGame
THE ESSENTIAL GUIDE TO SPECTATOR SPORT

This new series is designed to provide a complete overview of the major world sports for the rapidly-expanding spectator market, covering the history, the rules, the main terms, how the sport is played, the great stars and teams, the sport today and the future.

Intelligently written by leading sports journalists, the books are aimed at the passionate but discerning new sports fan. They take an alternative perspective to other sports titles, going beyond the normally bland observations and reflections of the commentator and professional sportsperson, providing readers with an informed and cliché-free framework within which to understand and appreciate the great sporting dramas.

Titles currently available:

Inside the Game: **Cricket** by Rob Steen
ISBN 1 84046 031 8

Inside the Game: **Golf** by Derek Lawrenson
ISBN 1 84046 030 X

Inside the Game: **Football** by Chris Nawrat
ISBN 1 84046 028 8

Inside the Game: **Boxing** by Harry Mullan
ISBN 1 84046 029 6

Titles for 1999:

Rugby Union, Formula 1, Horse Racing

INDEX

Ahmed, Mushtaq 167–8
Akram, Wasim 167
all out 7
all-rounders 13
amateur game 7–8
apartheid 102–3
Ashes 9–10, 87–91, 93–4, 95–8, 127, 132
Australia 118–19
    Second Test 1994 93–4
    Third Test 1981 87–91
    v West Indies 99
    Wisden World Championship 150

bails 6, 33–4
ball 11
    handling 36–7
    hit twice 37
    new 50–1
    swing 60–2
    tampering with 24–5
Barnes, Sydney 165
batting
    average 10
    crease 29
    order 13
    see also innings
beamer 21, 24
Benson & Hedges Cup 133
Bodyline 124–6
Botham, Ian 164
bouncer 25–6, 77–8
bowling 6, 11, 29–31, 32
    average 10
    crease 29
    overarm 106
    see also beamer; bouncer
Boycott, Geoff 51–2, 58
Bradman, Don 11, 13, 71–4, 86, 123–4, 163
Brearley, Mike 12, 90–2
bribery 17–18
bye 40–1

captains 14–16, 84–6, 113
catch 14, 31
Chappell, Ian 84–5, 135–6
class in cricket 112–14

covers 41
crease see batting crease; bowling crease; popping crease; return crease
cricket
    amateur 7–8
    class system 112–14
    origins 12, 101

delivery 6, 29–31
dismissal 31–8
D'Oliveira, Basil 102
duck 38, 52

England and Wales Cricket Board (ECB) 38, 69–70

fatalities 26, 39, 103
fielders 7, 41–3
first-class cricket 6

Gavaskar, Sunil 163
Gillette Cup 133
Grace, W.G. 104

Headingley 87
    matches 55–6, 95–8, 107–9, 115–7, 128–9, 144–8, 159–62
Headley, George 164
Healy, Ian 167
history 101
Hutton, Len 163

ICC 45, 139
innings 6, 7
    declaration 28–9
    totals 8–9

Jardine, Douglas 124–6
Jayasuriya, Sayanath 166
John Player Sunday League 133

Knott, Alan 82, 164–5

Lara, Brian 75–6, 166
Larwood, Harold 124–7
late cut 74–5

lbw 32–3
leg
   -bye 41
   side 6, 29
Lillee, Dennis 12–13, 77–8, 165
Lord's cricket ground 47

maiden 69
match examples 87
   see also under Headingley
MCC 38, 46
McGrath, Glenn 168
middle
   -order 13
   stump 29
Midwinter, Billy 154–5

night cricket 142
no ball 40
not out 11

obstructing the field 35–6
off side 6, 29
on side see leg side
one-day cricket 7, 8, 134
Oval, the 22
overarm bowling 106
overs 7–8, 27–8

Packer, Kerry 134–41, 150
pitch 6, 26–7, 53–6
popping crease 29, 57

Ranjitsinjhi, Prince 74–5
return crease 29
Richards, Viv 163–4
rubber 10
running on the pitch 26–7
run out 33–4, 45–6
runs 6, 7, 10–11

seamers 30, 79–80
sledging 25
slips 41
slow over rates 27–8
snick rule 33
Sobers, Gary 164

South Africa 102–3, 121
spin bowling 31, 35, 80–2
Stewart, Alec 13
sticky wicket 68
strike threat 130
stumped 35
stumps 29

Taylor, Mark 166
TCCB 38, 139
television rights 134–5, 141
Tendulkar, Sachin 166
Test cricket 6, 10, 156
   Australia v W Indies 99
   first official 121
   results 149
   see also Ashes
Thorpe, Graham 166–7
throwing 18–21
tie 7
timed out 37–8

Warne, Shane 80–2, 153, 167
Waugh, Steve 167
West Indies 91–2, 100, 150–1, 152–3
wicket 6, 7–8
   hit w. 35
wicketkeeper 6, 82–4
Wisden Cricketers' Almanack 131
Wisden Trophy 132
Women's Cricket Association 69–70
World Cup 45, 69, 134, 148, 155
World Series Cricket 135, 140–1
Worrell, Frank 14, 151

Zimbabwe 101–2, 121